Science
Puzzle Aid

KEY STAGE 4

SCIENCE

Supplementary Puzzles

MARTIN H. WILLIAMS B.Sc., M.A.

foulsham

LONDON • NEW YORK • TORONTO • SYDNEY

THE AUTHOR

Martin Williams B.Sc., M.A. has wide experience as a science teacher and has taught in Barclay Comprehensive School, Stevenage, Hayling Comprehensive School, Hampshire as co-head of Science and Ensham Girls' Comprehensive School, ILEA as Head of Science. In addition he was Senior Teacher and Curriculum Co-ordinator at Colne High School, Essex. Currently he is Deputy Head Teacher at Cotham Grammar School, Bristol. His teaching range covers science at all levels, Physics and Integrated Science to GCSE level and Biology, Chemistry and Psychology to 'A' level.

He has had a lifetime interest in puzzles and games and is of the firm opinion that learning should be fun. Through the puzzles in this book and the others of the series he hopes to make learning an enjoyable experience.

foulsham
Yeovil Road, Slough, Berkshire SL1 4JH

ISBN 0-572-01831-2

Illustrations by Elaine Hill, Mike Mosedale and Alisa Tingley.

Printed in Great Britain at St. Edmundsbury Press, Bury St. Edmunds.

CONTENTS

MATERIALS AND THEIR PROPERTIES

PHYSICAL PROCESSES

GENERAL

INTRODUCTION

WAYS TO USE THIS BOOK

As a learning aid

This book is best used as a study aid while you are working through the subject. Once you have completed a topic, the puzzles offer a good opportunity to test the depth of your knowledge. By attempting the whole topic without referring to the answers at the back of the book, you can identify where your knowledge is weak; you can then restudy your school notes or textbook in order to strengthen it.

Even before you have covered a topic in class you can use the clues and answers to identify the important elements within it. The puzzles can focus your attention on those key components which you will need to learn and remember.

As a revision aid

The best way to find out if you really know and understand something is to test yourself. And that is what you can do with these puzzles.

As your examinations get closer you should use the puzzles to ensure that you have all the facts you will need to be successful. Or to identify those areas where you are weak and need to spend your valuable revision time. The puzzles will enable you to do that — and in this way they really do increase your chances of a higher grade.

Work through all the puzzles and answer every question you can. You will then be able to mark yourself on each topic and learn exactly where your knowledge is strong or, more importantly, where it is weak. Revise your weakest topics first to bring them up to strength and then top up on your stronger areas.

Ideally, you should revise from your notes and textbooks but you will find that careful study of the questions and their answers can also be very helpful. Wherever you have found that you continually fail to solve a clue it might be worth filling in the answer in red, to remind yourself of the need to revise it more thoroughly as the examination gets closer.

If you use a pencil the puzzles can be attempted more than once.

TIPS TO HELP YOU

1. Read the instructions carefully.

2. Read through the clues and start with the easiest; this often helps you with others.

3. Some puzzles have Extra Clues (Puzzle 17) or a Reference Check (Puzzle 48) or Diagonals (Puzzle 10). If you really get stuck, but don't want to look up the whole answer, look up the answers to just these parts of the puzzle.

4. Have rough paper ready to jot down possible answers and try out spellings, etc.

5. If you want to start with an easy puzzle, try *Word Blocks*. If you like a challenge, try a *Solve and Fit* or *The Wheel*.

6. If after trying a puzzle you find you really can't finish it, look up the answers and write them in. The completed puzzle will then be useful as a reminder and as an aid for revision.

Other books in this series

There are *four* books in the Science Puzzle Aid series to completely cover the National Curriculum for Key Stage 4.

The other three books are:

BIOLOGY Puzzle Aid
(Life and Living Processes)   0-572-01828-2

CHEMISTRY Puzzle Aid
(Materials and their properties)   0-572-01829-0

PHYSICS Puzzle Aid
(Physical Processes)   0-572-01830-4

Quote the above book number when ordering from your bookseller and in case of difficulty ring foulsham on 0753-526769.

Solve the clues and place your answers in their correct positions in the grid. The questions can be about anything in biology. The first letters of several answers are already filled in.

13 letters — the process by which plants lose water into the atmosphere.

12 letters — this process leads either to growth of an organism or to the production of gametes. (4,8)

10 letters — the crab is this; it belongs to the class of invertebrates having between four and twenty pairs of legs.

— this consists of 79% nitrogen.

9 letters — to do this to blood means to put oxygen into it, as happens at the alveoli in the lungs.

— the earthworm grips its partner with this part of its body.

8 letters — this type of air contains more oxygen and less carbon dioxide than the air we breathe out.

7 letters — skull joints allowing little or no movement between the bones.

— type of vegetative reproduction organ found in the iris in which the stem stays underground for several years producing new buds.

— a collection of petals.

— another name for the pupa stage of an insect's life-cycle.

6 letters — the palisade cells of these plant parts are the site of photosynthesis.

— bees, ants and termites are examples of this type of insect.

— this is present in R.N.A., but not D.N.A., and can join to adenine.

— the surname of the monk who studied genetics.

— the _ _ _ _ _ _ _ _ formula for humans is written
$$I\tfrac{2}{2}\ C\tfrac{1}{1}\ PM\tfrac{2}{2}\ M\tfrac{3}{3}.$$

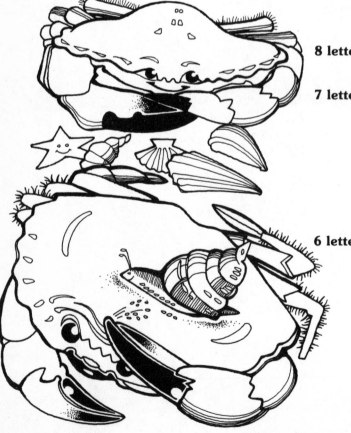

5 letters — the type of neurone which carries an impulse to a muscle or gland.

— the eating stage of an insect's life-cycle which shows complete metamorphosis.

— a secretion of some plants, e.g. pine.

— ones made of cartilage separate the vertebrae.

— another word to describe a person's characteristic.

4 letters — the _ _ _ _ BIOTIC penicillin is an example of a chemical secreted by bacteria or fungi which is used by man to kill other micro-organisms.

— a word to describe drainage in clay soils.

— the artery called the aorta leads out of this ventricle.

— adenine and thymine are an example of a _ _ _ _ pair.

— the coracoid bones of a bird transmit this to the wings.

3 letters — the abbreviated name of a plant hormone involved in growth.

An ABC of Biology

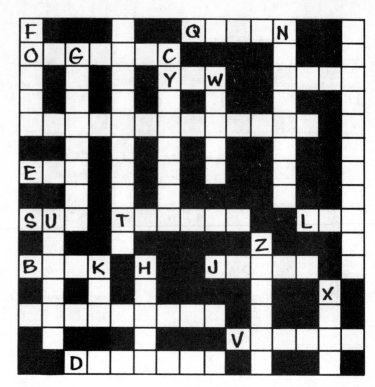

This puzzle consists of twenty-six clues. Each one begins with a different letter of the alphabet. Solve the clues and arrange the answers in the correct pattern. The positions of most of the answers are given to start you off.

A The ability of the lens of the eye to change its shape when it switches from looking at close to distant objects. (13)

B Darwin found that the finches on the Galapagos Islands all had different types of this. (4)

C This base bonds to guanine in D.N.A. (8)

D A word to describe the condition of seeds when they are waiting for the right conditions for germination. (7)

E The female gamete in plants and animals. (3)

F The part of the retina which contains only cones and gives the most accurate image. (5)

G This chemical is the form in which energy is stored in the liver and muscles. (8)

H The scar on a seed formed when the ovule detaches from the ovary. (5)

I An insect is called this when the stages of its metamorphosis are egg-nymph-adult. (10)

J A movable one is called synovial. (5)

K A series of questions used to identify an unknown organism. (3)

L The _ _ _ _ ERAL line of a fish contains hair cells which detect movement. (3)

M Radiation can cause chromosomes to change in this way MU _ _ _ _ _. (4)

N The element that is excreted from the body in the urine. (8)

O These kinds of compounds all contain carbon. (7)

P A tapeworm must receive its food in this condition because it has no digestive enzymes of its own. (11)

Q The only fertile female in the bee colony. (5)

R The process which involves materials being used more than once because they are too valuable to throw away. (9)

S The source of all energy on the planet Earth. (3)

T The number of teeth humans have in their first set. (6)

U The tube which carries urine from the kidney to the bladder. (6)

V An example of continuous _ _ _ _ _ _ ION in a population is the complete range of people's height or weight. (6)

W The largest living mammal. (5)

X A type of radiation which can cause the M clue to happen. (1,3)

Y When fish do this from side to side it is because of damage to their ventral or dorsal fins. (3)

Z The shape of a male stickleback's courtship dance. (3,3)

THE WHEEL

All the answers are five-letter words, starting at the outside and working inwards. When complete, the outer circle will contain words to do with digestion. The inner circle will contain a jumble of letters. Sort them out to make two words of 4 letters and 12 letters, which will be the things the outer circle words help to digest.

1 Liquid produced to help keep us cool.
2 Artery leading from heart.
3 Organ receiving the most blood per minute.
4 Adult insect.
5 External opening of vagina.
6 These conduct impulses away from the cell body.
7 A type of connecting neurone.
8 Fungus which can ferment sugar.
9 Most people have about five litres of this.
10 This part of the ear is filled with fluids.
11 Water can do this to the soil's minerals (i.e. wash them out).
12 Digestion occurs _____-cellularly in saprophytes.
13 A _____ is a person of very short stature because they have too little pituitary growth hormone.
14 Excretory fluid.
15 Good soil has a _____-like structure.
16 Excess amino-acids removed in 14 are this.

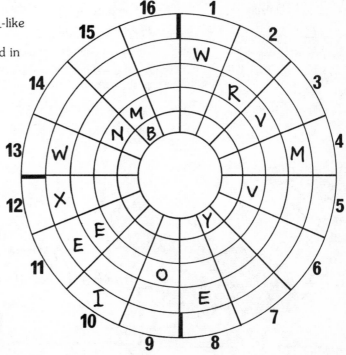

Missing Letters

The answers to these clues are jumbled up and each answer has one missing letter. Write the correct word, then put the letter which was missing into the lefthand column. When these letters are read downwards they spell the names of male reproductive glands.

1 _P_ DHILAO   The number of chromosomes in a gamete is called this. _Haploid_

  _R_ CCAADI   The sphincter where the oesphagus meets the stomach. _Cardiac_

  _O_ BMB   The type of calorimeter used to measure the energy content of food. _Bom_

  _S_ SEAOORL   Use of these is breaking down the ozone layer of the atmosphere. _Aeros_

  ____ RLERIOAES   These blood vessels connect the capillaries to the arteries. _____

  ____ TP   The "energy molecule" of the cells, written in an abbreviated form. _____

  ____ ATCAYLS   Enzymes are examples of this because they speed up the chemical _____
                   reactions of digestion.

  ____ LGFALLA   Some bacteria have these to help them move. _____

2 ____ AHNRAID   This class contains spiders. _____

  ____ ABRD   The shape of most leaves is this to increase surface area. _____

  ____ TORHG   This part of an organism's development is controlled by hormones. ____

  ____ ROC   When different plants are grown on the same land in successive years, it
                   called _____ rotation. _____

  ____ DODNUUM   The region of the digestive system which receives secretions from
                   the pancreas and gall bladder. _____

  _R_ SBAB   These branch off from the shaft of a feather. _BARBS_ _____

  ____ NAU   The faeces are pushed out through this. _____

AARGGH   yuuuk

12

3 ____ TYC   In adverse or difficult conditions, amoeba can form this. _____

____ MCHY   The creamy, partly-digested fluid which leaves the stomach. _____

____ NOIA   Proteins are broken down into these acids. _____

____ SACLURE   There are two of these chambers in the heart. _____

____ IENAC   Sharp, pointed "killing" tooth. _____

____ HD   Abbreviation for the hormone which controls the amount of water in urine. _____

____ BBU   A vegetative reproductive organ which is a swollen stem, as used by the daffodil. _____

____ REXIC   The narrow entrance to the womb. _____

____ ROXTC   These plant cells store starch. _____

____ MLIFEYU   Bile does this to fat — splits it into droplets _____

____ LAX   This bud forms in the angle between a leaf and a stem of a plant. _____

____ BACONIVE   The shape of a red blood cell. _____

____ YAXC   This part of a flower is made up of sepals _____

____ SGITD   Enzymes do this to food so that it can be absorbed into the bloodstream. _____

4 ____ GINESOE   The passing out of undigested food. _____

____ RACIS   A disease causing holes to form in the teeth. _____

____ HIF   These vertebrates are poikilothermic, live in water and lay eggs. _____

____ DD   Abbreviation for a chemical, used as an insecticide, which became concentrated in food chains. _____

____ NEBNAIL   This type of plant does not flower in its first year, but develops large storage organs. _____

____ FAEL   The apple is an example of this type of fruit. _____

MISSING LETTERS

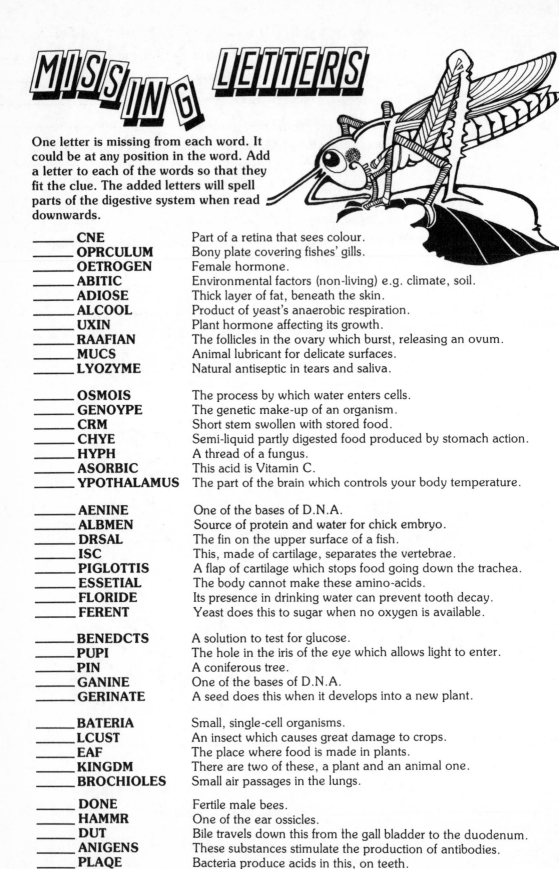

One letter is missing from each word. It could be at any position in the word. Add a letter to each of the words so that they fit the clue. The added letters will spell parts of the digestive system when read downwards.

Word	Clue
_____ CNE	Part of a retina that sees colour.
_____ OPRCULUM	Bony plate covering fishes' gills.
_____ OETROGEN	Female hormone.
_____ ABITIC	Environmental factors (non-living) e.g. climate, soil.
_____ ADIOSE	Thick layer of fat, beneath the skin.
_____ ALCOOL	Product of yeast's anaerobic respiration.
_____ UXIN	Plant hormone affecting its growth.
_____ RAAFIAN	The follicles in the ovary which burst, releasing an ovum.
_____ MUCS	Animal lubricant for delicate surfaces.
_____ LYOZYME	Natural antiseptic in tears and saliva.
_____ OSMOIS	The process by which water enters cells.
_____ GENOYPE	The genetic make-up of an organism.
_____ CRM	Short stem swollen with stored food.
_____ CHYE	Semi-liquid partly digested food produced by stomach action.
_____ HYPH	A thread of a fungus.
_____ ASORBIC	This acid is Vitamin C.
_____ YPOTHALAMUS	The part of the brain which controls your body temperature.
_____ AENINE	One of the bases of D.N.A.
_____ ALBMEN	Source of protein and water for chick embryo.
_____ DRSAL	The fin on the upper surface of a fish.
_____ ISC	This, made of cartilage, separates the vertebrae.
_____ PIGLOTTIS	A flap of cartilage which stops food going down the trachea.
_____ ESSETIAL	The body cannot make these amino-acids.
_____ FLORIDE	Its presence in drinking water can prevent tooth decay.
_____ FERENT	Yeast does this to sugar when no oxygen is available.
_____ BENEDCTS	A solution to test for glucose.
_____ PUPI	The hole in the iris of the eye which allows light to enter.
_____ PIN	A coniferous tree.
_____ GANINE	One of the bases of D.N.A.
_____ GERINATE	A seed does this when it develops into a new plant.
_____ BATERIA	Small, single-cell organisms.
_____ LCUST	An insect which causes great damage to crops.
_____ EAF	The place where food is made in plants.
_____ KINGDM	There are two of these, a plant and an animal one.
_____ BROCHIOLES	Small air passages in the lungs.
_____ DONE	Fertile male bees.
_____ HAMMR	One of the ear ossicles.
_____ DUT	Bile travels down this from the gall bladder to the duodenum.
_____ ANIGENS	These substances stimulate the production of antibodies.
_____ PLAQE	Bacteria produce acids in this, on teeth.
_____ LYPH	Tissue fluid after it has passed into the lymphatic system.

A MIX UP

A-M

The definitions of the following words have become confused. Can you sort them out? Put the pairs of letters and numbers in the grid provided.

ANTIGEN
AFTERBIRTH
ALKALINE
4 AMMONIA
5 BRONCHUS
6 BOWMAN'S
CAPSULE
7 CASEIN
8 CARNASSIAL
9 CHLOROPLAST
10 CONTINUOUS
11 CONJUNCTIVA
12 DIASTOLE
13 DIABETES
14 ENTERON
15 EVOLUTION
16 FAT
17 FILAMENT

18 FLOSS
19 GRAVITY
20 GASTRIC
21 GUARD CELLS

22 HEPATIC
   PORTAL
23 HERBIVORE
24 IMPULSES
25 ISLETS
26 JENNER
27 LACTASE
28 KILL
29 METHYLENE
   BLUE
30 MUCOR

A   Eats plants only.
B   A stain used to identify parts of animal cells.
C   Electrical ones are carried along nerve cells or neurones.
D   Hydrochloric acid is part of this fluid or secretion.
E   Transparent skin over the eyeball.
F   Can be converted to nitrates by nitrifying bacteria in the soil.

G   This vein carries blood from the intestines to the liver.
H   Two of these lead off the trachea in the lungs.
I   Collects the filtrate from the glomerulus in the kidney.
J   A shoot is negatively geotropic when it grows away from this.
K   The protein found in milk.
L   Large teeth used for cutting meat, found in dogs.
M   Found immediately to each side of a leaf stoma.
N   Contains the green pigment chlorophyll.
O   The placenta leaving the mother after the baby is born.
P   Provides 39kJ g when respired aerobically in our body.
Q   Process whereby species change gradually over millions of years.
R   The central gut of a hydra.
S   You can buy this to get food out from between your teeth.
T   _____ of Langerhans are found in the pancreas.
U   Part of the heart-beat when the ventricle is relaxed and filling with blood.
V   A foreign organism or chemical in the blood which stimulates the production of antibodies.
W   Opposite to an acid, with a pH of between 7 and 14.
X   The anther is on the end of this in a flower.
Y   Name of mould often found growing on bread.
Z   What many carnivorous animals do with their canine teeth.
a   The enzyme that digests milk sugar or lactose.
b   One of the first people to use a vaccine.
c   Weight differences in people are an example of this type of variation.
d   Disease where sugar is lost in the urine because insufficient insulin is produced by the pancreas.

A	B	C	D	E	F	G	H	I	J	K	L	M	N	O

P	Q	R	S	T	U	V	W	X	Y	Z	a	b	c	d

A Mix Up

N-Z

The definitions of the following words have
become confused. Can you sort them out?
Put the pairs of letters and numbers in the
grid provided.

A	B	C	D	E	F	G	H	I	J	K	L	M	N	O

P	Q	R	S	T	U	V	W	X	Y	Z	a	b	c	d

1 NOISE

2 NECTAR

3 NICTATING
   MEMBRANE

4 OXYHAEMOGLOBIN

5 OBESE

6 PELVIS

7 PHARYNX

8 PLASMA

9 POIKILOTHERMIC

10 PACINIAN
    CORPUSCLE

11 PITUITARY

12 QUARANTINE

13 RELAX

14 ROOT HAIRS

15 RADICLE

16 SCOLEX

17 STABILITY

18 SEDIMENTARY

19 SUCROSE

20 SYNOVIAL

21 THYROID

22 TIDAL VOLUME

23 TAPEWORM

24 ULNA

25 VITAL CAPACITY

26 VARIEGATED

27 VACUOLE

28 WEB

29 X-CHROMOSOME

30 ZYGOSPORE

A These increase the surface area available for a plant to absorb water.

B A space in a cell.

C A period when an animal is isolated to make sure it is disease-free.

D An endocrine gland producing many hormones.

E A sensory receptor in the skin which detects pressure.

F A pollution measured in decibels.

G The name of a young plant root.

H The liquid part of the blood.

I Insects collect this when they visit plants.

J Lots of connected food chains make a food _____.

K An inner eyelid found in the eyes of birds.

L The maximum volume of air you can force in or out in one breath.

M Made up of a thick wall round a zygote, e.g. spirogyra.

N The name of the chemical in a red blood cell after it has combined with oxygen.

O A gland in the neck which produces thyroxine.

P This word describes an animal whose body temperature changes with the environment (cold-blooded).

Q Describes a very overweight person.

R Males have one, females have two.

S This widens in girls at puberty.

T This consists of hooks and suckers which allow the tapeworm to attach itself to our gut wall.

U The back of the mouth.

V Muscle can do this when not contracted.

W An arm bone between the humerus and carpals.

X A moveable joint, e.g. hips or knees.

Y The volume of air exchanged with each breath.

Z Fins give this to fish.

a A green leaf that has some areas of no chlorophyll (white).

b A disaccharide made of glucose and fructose.

c Fossils are formed in this type of rock.

d A human parasite found in the gut.

First & Last

Answer the clues. When complete, the first letters of each answer read downwards will form two connected words to do with classification. So will the last letter of each answer.

Many such compounds are used for fertilisers.

A connecting neurone.

This leaves via the lachrymal duct.

_ _ _ _ _ _ _ _ _ _ _ S meaning constant internal body conditions.

Light-sensitive back of eye.

_ _ _ _ _ _ AROUS means groups that lay eggs.

This disease is characterised by paralysis.

Light-sensitive units of insect's compound eye are called _ _ _ _ _ _ _ _ IA.

Abbreviation for Deoxyribose Nucleic Acid.

Minute hair-like growths from cells.

Protein is needed for this body function.

This dissolved in water makes urine.

The male testes are protected by the scrotal _ _ _ _.

This sense is carried out by the Meissner's corpuscles of the skin.

The 'fight or flight' hormone.

Sound sensing part of cochlea.

This covers and protects the eye.

A single-celled animal.

Grid letters (given): M M / Y / E O / A / O / V / M M / I / R / O U / D / I / Y / B

TRIANGLES

Solve the clues and place the answers (all have five letters) into the spaces in the triangles below. The first and last letters of each word fit into the squares. For each clue, start at the first number and write towards the second number.

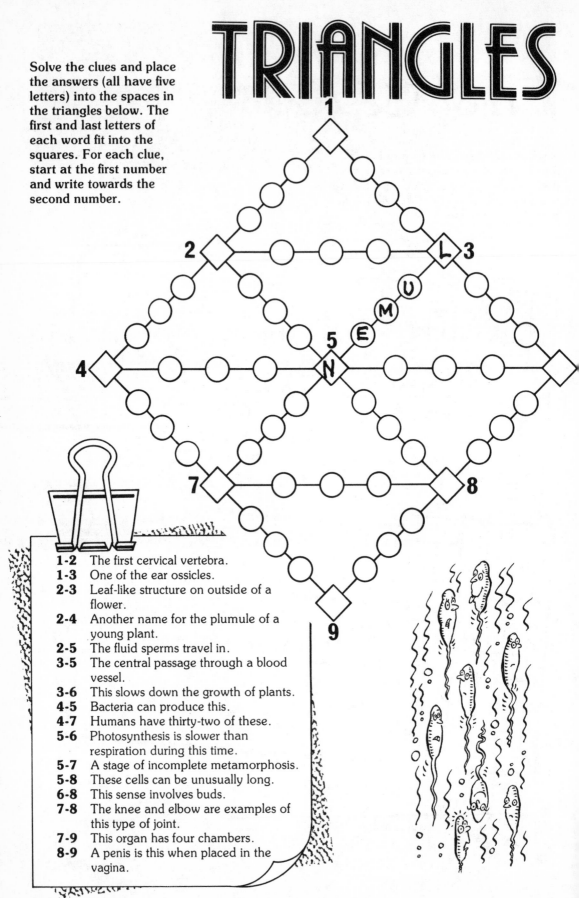

1-2   The first cervical vertebra.
1-3   One of the ear ossicles.
2-3   Leaf-like structure on outside of a flower.
2-4   Another name for the plumule of a young plant.
2-5   The fluid sperms travel in.
3-5   The central passage through a blood vessel.
3-6   This slows down the growth of plants.
4-5   Bacteria can produce this.
4-7   Humans have thirty-two of these.
5-6   Photosynthesis is slower than respiration during this time.
5-7   A stage of incomplete metamorphosis.
5-8   These cells can be unusually long.
6-8   This sense involves buds.
7-8   The knee and elbow are examples of this type of joint.
7-9   This organ has four chambers.
8-9   A penis is this when placed in the vagina.

WORD BLOCKS

Answer the clues. A word will be formed diagonally across the block. Each diagonal has something to do with classification.

A   DIAGONAL There is a plant one and an animal one.

1   The material which gives animal skin its waterproofing properties.
2   The glomerulus of the kidney does this to blood.
3   This part of the vertebrae makes red blood cells.
4   The cell bodies of the neurones produce these swellings in the dorsal root of the spinal cord.
5   Where urine is stored in the body.
6   Wearing away of rock caused by wind or rain.
7   The growth of a plant root in the direction of gravity is called positive GEO_ _ _ _ _ _ _ _ .

B   DIAGONAL In man this level of classification is given the name primate.

1   This organ produces eggs in the female mammal.
2   Zinc, copper and magnesium are examples of this type of element which are needed in minute amounts by plants and animals.
3   The site in the lymph system where white blood cells are produced.
4   The chamber of a ruminant's stomach which is home to bacteria which help with the digestion of cellulose.
5   The pinna are in this part of the ear.

See over

C DIAGONAL Felidae is the name of the _____ commonly known as cats.

1 The name of the waste product egested from the body.
2 This digestive juice contains amylase.
3 This material sets the teeth into the gums.
4 An image is formed on this part of the eye.
5 This type of blood vessel connects capillaries to veins.
6 The useful product of aerobic and anaerobic respiration.

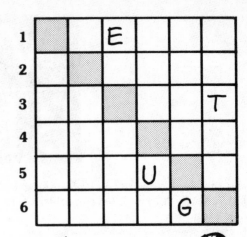

D DIAGONAL A group of organisms with many similarities but which cannot all interbreed successfully.

1 Fungi are unusual plants because they are not this colour.
2 Bacteria cause this to happen to dead organic matter.
3 This type of soil has very good drainage because of large air spaces between the particles.
4 This organism has a protein coat around its D.N.A.
5 This syndrome is caused by an extra chromosome.

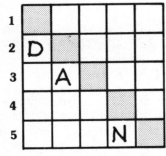

E DIAGONAL Mammalia is an example of this level of classification.

1 Enamel is deposited in this part of the tooth.
2 The _ _ _ _ spot on the retina is found where the optic nerve leaves for the brain.
3 In the fluid-filled cavities of the utriculus are gelatinous plates containing granules of this substance.
4 This type of pollination involves two flowers.
5 These are made mostly from calcium phosphate.

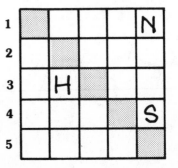

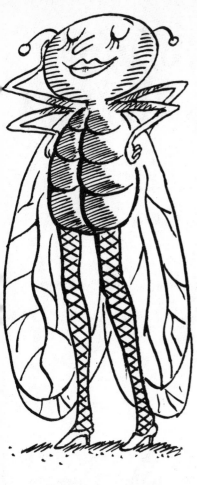

F   DIAGONAL A group of organisms capable of interbreeding.

1   A section of an earthworm's body or an insect's leg.
2   This sticks to the outer surface of bacteria to make it easier for the white cells to ingest them.
3   The type of reproduction which does not involve gametes.
4   The windpipe.
5   A small chain of amino-acids — not long enough to be a protein.
6   The state of blood vessels when the body is too hot.
7   Disease caused by lack of Vitamin D.

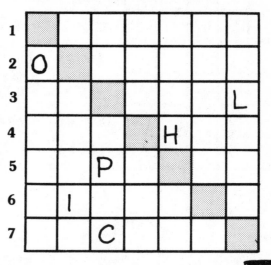

G   DIAGONAL Vertebrata is an example of this level of classification.

1   The wider this girdle is the easier a woman will find it to give birth.
2   We do this to produce heat when we are cold.
3   This gas makes up 20% of the atmosphere.
4   This type of nervous action does not involve the brain.
5   The part of the alimentary canal where faeces collect before being pushed out through the anus.
6   The vessels which conduct food in a plant.

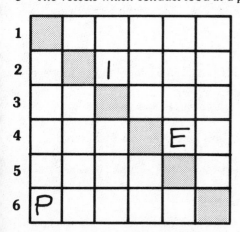

The first letter of Clue 1, the second letter of Clue 2, and so on, read diagonally give the names of a disease caused by lack of certain nutrients.

A

What the eye lens does to light.

These muscles can alter the shape of the eye lens.

Fats pass from this into the lymphatic system.

Can cause lung cancer.

One of the glands in the male reproductive system.

These allow the exchange of gases in a leaf.

The controller of a cell.

B

The parts of the lung concerned with gaseous exchange.

Chisel-shaped tooth.

Twisted strands of albumen supporting yolk of egg.

The gland which produces adrenalin.

Amylase and pepsin are examples of these.

Diabetics lack this to control their blood sugar.

A type of water flea.

C

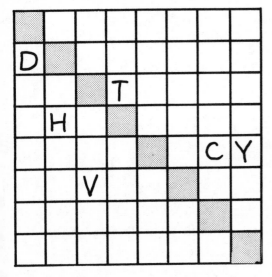

It is important that your diet is this.

This kind of a smear is used to check for cancer in women.

In gliding, the wings of a bird are outspread to act like this.

This protects against antigens.

Brain centre for memory.

Butterflies are an example of this type of metamorphosis.

This nerve connects the ear to the brain.

A small structure within the nucleus.

D

This kind of organism lives in or on its host.

This fibre conducts impulses to the cell body of a nerve.

Fluid that has collected in the Bowman's capsule of the kidney.

Finger bone.

Air-bladders give bony fish control of this.

A lens does this to light to correct short sight.

The osmotic _____ is a measure of a cell's ability to draw in water.

Area of uterus wall very rich in blood.

E

The tough outer coat around the eyball.

A characteristic of fish.

Ligaments and muscles are attached to this part of the vertebrae.

Where the baby develops inside its mother.

A form of transport that requires energy.

_____-two, the number of teeth that humans have.

Transfer all the numbers of the letters you use to answer the clues to the Reference Check, and then to the crossword. A biological message will be formed. Also, the first letter of each answer will spell out a famous scientist and the theory that he is famous for.

Biological Message

Reference Check

1	2	3	4	5	6	7	8	9	10	11	12	13	14	15	16	17	18	19	20	21

Clue	Numbers
A type of nutrient.	1, 2, 7, 3, 6, 11, 12, 4, 7, 2, 5, 8.
Factor affecting rate of transpiration.	11, 9, 10, 13, 4, 13, 5, 12.
The digestive canal.	2, 14, 13, 10, 8, 15, 5, 2, 7, 12.
To do this is a characteristic of life.	7, 8, 16, 7, 6, 4, 9, 1, 8.
These have nodules full of bacteria.	14, 8, 17, 9, 10, 8, 18.
Insect sheds its skin.	8, 1, 4, 12, 18, 13, 18
Number of kilojoules in 1g of carbohydrate.	18, 8, 19, 8, 15, 5, 8, 8, 15
Getting rid of solid wastes.	4, 8, 20, 8, 1, 2, 5, 13, 6, 15
Roots growing directly from stem.	2, 4, 19, 8, 15, 5, 13, 5, 13, 6, 9, 18
Horizontal underground stem which reproduces vegetatively.	7, 11, 13, 21, 6, 10, 8, 18
This tube can expand 400 times when a woman is pregnant.	22, 6, 10, 3
Site of much absorption and digestion.	13, 15, 5, 8, 18, 5, 13, 15, 8, 18
Nectar stores in flowering plants.	15, 8, 1, 5, 2, 7, 12
The type of waste excreted in the urine.	15, 13, 5, 7, 6, 17, 8, 15, 6, 9, 18
The third stage of mitosis.	2, 15, 2, 16, 11, 2, 18, 8
Humans have thirty-two of these.	5, 8, 8, 5, 11
This tube takes urine out through the penis.	9, 7, 8, 5, 11, 7, 2
A nutrient important for peristalsis.	7, 6, 9, 17, 11, 2, 17, 8
The largest group of invertebrates.	2, 7, 5, 11, 7, 6, 16, 6, 4
The green variety of these can photosynthesise.	14, 8, 2, 20
Type of pollination involving only one plant.	18, 8, 14, 20
These plants have leaves adapted to reduce transpiration.	8, 19, 8, 7, 17, 7, 8, 8, 15
A fluid similar to plasma, but with fewer proteins.	14, 12, 10, 16, 11
The outer layer of skin.	8, 16, 13, 4, 8, 7, 10, 13, 18
Another name for the collar bone.	1, 14, 2, 19, 13, 1, 14, 8
The insect which carries sleeping sickness.	5, 18, 8, 5, 18, 8
A group of flowers on a main stalk.	13, 15, 20, 14, 6, 7, 8, 18, 1, 8, 15,
Tube from mouth to stomach.	6, 8, 18, 6, 16, 11, 2, 17, 9, 18
Bacteria forming nitrates in the soil.	15, 13, 5, 7, 13, 20, 12, 13, 15, 17

TRUE OR FALSE

Just write F for false or T for true at the end of each
statement.

1 Water sticking to the walls of xylem is an example of adhesion.
2 Adenosine triphosphate contains two molecules of phosphate.
3 The tarsal bones make up the ankle of the foot.
4 A plant which flowers every two years is called an annual.
5 Earthworms reproduce by binary fission.
6 The sternum is the correct term for the breast bone.
7 Animals have cell walls made of cellulose.
8 Acetyl choline is a chemical which passes across synapses of the nervous system.
9 Chains of amino-acids are called fats.
10 Chlorine is added to our toothpaste.
11 Clay soils are poorly aerated compared to sandy soils.
12 The final or tail vertebra is called the coccyx.
13 A converging lens is needed to correct long sight.
14 The brain can be called the cranium.
15 Animals which only eat plants are called decomposers.
16 The duck-billed platypus is an egg-laying mammal.
17 The endoplasmic reticulum is the transport system of the cell.
18 Evaporation is the method by which water leaves the plant's leaf through the stomata.
19 Getting rid of waste in the faeces is called excretion.
20 The inner ear is fluid-filled.
21 Geotropism is a plant's response to light.
22 Homozygous means, for example, having the same colour hair from both parents.
23 Bee cells in their hives have five sides.
24 The kidney receives blood from the hepatic artery.
25 Ingest means to take food into the body.
26 The adipose layer of the skin provides insulation.
27 Lime flocculates a clay soil, causing its particles to stick together.
28 Mitosis is the process which occurs when cells divide in the ovary or testis.
29 Sperms are mobile because they have tails.
30 The ear has oval, square and round windows.

26

Answer Clues 1-12, using the groups of letters provided. The word beginnings are underlined. (Not all the groups will be used to fill the Answer Grid.) When you have finished, the name of a famous scientist will be revealed by reading down the first column. The remaining groups of letters can be arranged to describe this scientist.

ANSWER GRID

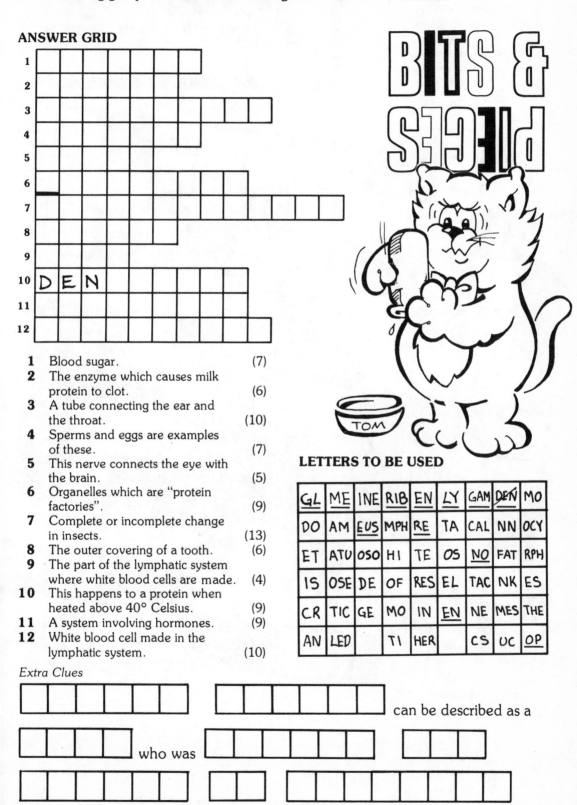

1   Blood sugar.   (7)
2   The enzyme which causes milk protein to clot.   (6)
3   A tube connecting the ear and the throat.   (10)
4   Sperms and eggs are examples of these.   (7)
5   This nerve connects the eye with the brain.   (5)
6   Organelles which are "protein factories".   (9)
7   Complete or incomplete change in insects.   (13)
8   The outer covering of a tooth.   (6)
9   The part of the lymphatic system where white blood cells are made.   (4)
10   This happens to a protein when heated above 40° Celsius.   (9)
11   A system involving hormones.   (9)
12   White blood cell made in the lymphatic system.   (10)

LETTERS TO BE USED

GL	ME	INE	RIB	EN	LY	GAM	DEN	MO
DO	AM	EUS	MPH	RE	TA	CAL	NN	OCY
ET	ATU	OSO	HI	TE	OS	NO	FAT	RPH
IS	OSE	DE	OF	RES	EL	TAC	NK	ES
CR	TIC	GE	MO	IN	EN	NE	MES	THE
AN	LED		TI	HER		CS	UC	OP

Extra Clues

[ ][ ][ ][ ][ ][ ][ ] [ ][ ][ ][ ][ ][ ][ ] can be described as a

[ ][ ][ ][ ][ ] who was [ ][ ][ ][ ][ ][ ] [ ][ ][ ]

[ ][ ][ ][ ][ ][ ][ ][ ] [ ][ ] [ ][ ][ ][ ][ ][ ]

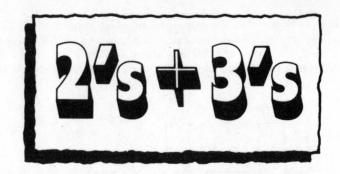

Complete the crossword in the normal way. However, your answers must be written with two or three letters in each square. There is only one single letter, which is already filled in. No other single letters are used.

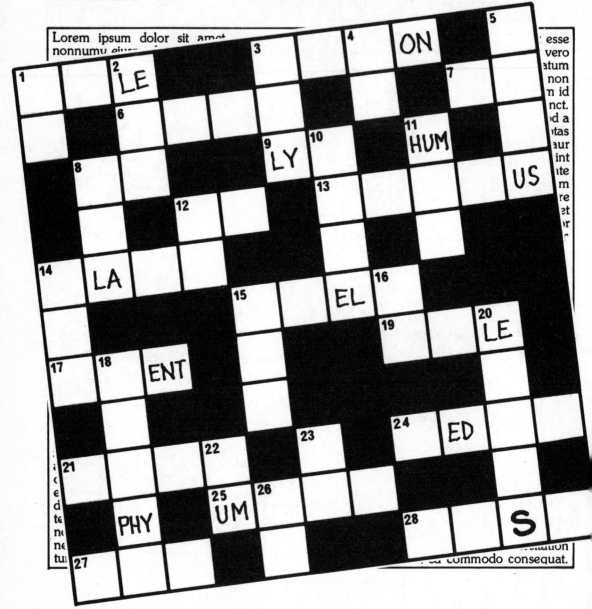

CLUES ACROSS

1 Gene controlling a characteristic, e.g. T represents tallness. (6)
3 Can cause mutations. (9)
6 The appendix is an example of this type of organ. (9)
7 Round bacteria. (5)
8 Coniferous trees. (4)
9 A type of antibody which destroys bacteria by dissolving their outer coats. (5)
12 Small insect which feeds on plant juices that it sucks from leaves and stems. (5)
13 There are about one million "knots of capillaries" in the kidney. (10)
14 This absorbs oxygen in a bird's egg. (9)
15 The earthworm grips its partner with this. (9)
17 Holds bones together at the joints. (8)
19 Part of a feather which has hooks. (7)
21 The plumule's protective sheath (10)
24 Solution used to test for sugars. (9)
25 The cord attaching baby to mother. (9)
27 Vessel leading away from the heart. (6)
28 Antagonistic to the tricuspid muscle (8)

CLUES DOWN

1 Phylum of plant found in water (5)
2 Ear ossicles act in this way. (6)
3 A flower which can be cut along many vertical planes to produce identical halves. (8)
4 The type of symmetrical movement detected by the utriculus in the ear. (4)
5 A rod-shaped bacterium. (8)
8 Leg bone between the femur and tarsals. (6)
10 An amoeba consists of a
_ _ _ _ _ _ _ _ _ L. (9)
11 Funny arm bone. (7)
12 Part of the Latin name for the honey bee. (4)
14 The lung's air sacs. (7)
15 Example of a legume. (6)
16 Five vertebrae in the small of the back. (6)
18 This generation of moss or fern reproduces sexually. (12)
20 Pores in bark. (9)
22 Small intestines. (5)
23 These increase the surface area of 22 Down. (5)
26 This emulsifies fats and is stored in the gall bladder. (4)

Twos
and
Threes

Complete the crossword in the normal way. However, your answers must be written with two or three letters in each square. Six single letters have been already filled in. No other single letters have been used.

CLUES ACROSS
2 The antagonistic pair to the tricep muscle. (5)
4 This stores urine. (7)
5 An enlarged specialised part of the spinal cord. (5)
7 The first vertebra taking the weight of the skull. (5)
9 This chemical is responsible for reducing the volume of urine produced. (4,8,7)
13 The liver converts nitrogen into this because it is less poisonous. (4)
14 The process by which the bonds in proteins, fat and carbohydrate are broken (10)
16 One of these would be identical to you. (5)
17 _ _ _ _ _ _ _ _ _ _ _ US fish have no bones. (11)
19 A double one is the shape of D.N.A. (5)
20 and 21 Down. Bulbs, corms, rhizomes and tubers are examples of this. (7)(5)
23 Sebum from the sebaceous glands keeps the skin like this. (6)
25 Alternative name for the large intestine. (5)
26 This organ breaks down red blood cells. (6)
27 This cord and the brain make up a vertebrate's nervous system. (6)
29 This pollutant can cause brain damage and is found in petrol. (4)
31 A stage of an insect's life if it shows incomplete metamorphosis. (5)
32 A nerve linking the ear to the brain. (8)
33 Three letters representing the name of the chemical that chromosomes are made of. (3)

CLUES DOWN
1 Worms improve this soil property by burrowing. (8)
3 Sperms are stored here. (10)
4 A test for protein. (6)
6 The other name for this ear ossicle is the anvil. (5)
8 _ _ _ _ILOTHERMIC means warm-blooded. (4)
10 Lower incisors bite against this pad in a sheep's mouth. (5)
11 A nerve cell. (7)
12 An animal supported by fluid and not bone is said to have one. (13)
15 The other name for this ear ossicle is the stapes. (7)
16 A slowly revolving machine used in tropism experiments is called _ _ _ _ _ _ _ AT. (7)
18 BACTERIO _ _ _ _ _ are viruses which attack bacteria. (5)
21 See 20 Across (5)
22 This projection or mound can be found on a molar tooth. (4)
23 A type of 11 down. (7)
24 This cavity is fluid-filled between the lungs and ribs. (7)
25 Ants, bees and termites are examples of animals which live in such a group. (6)
30 Imago is the other way of describing this insect stage. (5)

DOUBLE puzzle

Answer as many clues as you can, and fill in the Answer Grid. Then transfer the numbered letters to the Reference Check and then to the Message Grid. When this Grid is partly filled in, you may be able to work out its missing letters. So transfer these letters to the Reference Grid and the Answer Grid. This will give you extra help towards any unanswered clues. When you read down the first column of the Answer Grid, two words to do with animal nutrition will be made. (There are Extra Clues for these.) The Message Grid will give information about the skeleton.

ANSWER GRID

CLUES

1 The tail fin of a fish. (6)
2 Respiration involving oxygen. (7)
3 First part of a cow's four-chambered stomach. (5)
4 An amphibian. (4)
5 Soft organs are protected from this by the skeleton. (6)
6 Smaller than bacteria, causes disease, e.g. influenza. (5)
7 Layer of the stratosphere which is breaking down due to the use of aerosols. (5)
8 The type of jelly a queen bee eats all her life. (5)
9 Bile does this to fat. (8)
10 Mammals rear their offspring on this. (4)
11 A fluid found in the inner ear. (9)
12 Nutrient jelly on which bacteria can grow. (4)
13 CHEMO_ _ _ _ _ is how an amoeba senses food. (5)

Extra Clues

Clues for the two words to do with animal nutrition in the first column.
1 An animal which does not eat plants. (9)
2 What the above animal does eat. (4)

Reference Check

1	2	3	4	5	6	7	8	9	10	11	12	13	14	15	16	17	18	19	20	21	22	23	24	25

Message Grid

These words have been jumbled up. (There are no letters missing.) Luckily clues have been left. Put the correct spelling in the space provided.

1	OWRKRE	-sterile female bees	_____
2	SLWIT	-a plant will do this when water is not available	_____
3	IAVIMTNS	-needed in the diet to maintain good health	_____
4	IVNE	-carries blood to the heart	_____
5	GIVAAN	-external opening to the female reproductive tract	_____
6	EDNTNO	-attaches muscle to bone	_____
7	TSIYPRN	-enzyme found in the duodenum	_____
8	ROHTPIC	- food chains are made up of different _ _ _ _ _ _ _ levels	_____
9	OGNUET	- this organ has taste buds	_____
10	GITRUD	-describes a "full" cell	_____
11	SSATEP	-another name for the ossicle called the stirrup	_____
12	OMSCATH	-pepsin and rennin are enzymes which work here	_____
13	TASEE	-bristles used during movement by the earthworm	_____
14	GYSOPN	- the type of leaf mesophyll with lots of air spaces	_____
15	AASRCL	- five vertebrae which are fused or joined	_____
16	PNICTSHRE	-cardiac, pyloric and anal are all examples of this	_____
17	RBSI	- these move upwards and outwards during respiration	_____
18	RIDASU	- arm bone between humerus and carpals	_____
19	BREPUYT	- a time of rapid growth and development in boys and girls	_____
20	EULPS	- this has the same rate as the heart-beat	_____
21	LOPAMURNY	- this vein and artery connect the lungs and heart	_____
22	TERPMOETO	-equipment used to measure transpiration in plants	_____
23	NCPEARAS	- a diffuse organ where insulin is made	_____
24	YRMIAPDOS	- these belong to the phylum Arthropoda along with Insects, Arachnids and Crustacea	_____
25	LIMEYCUM	- a lot of fungal hyphae	_____
26	EAMLSY	- pork's appearance when it contains tapeworm	_____
27	OAML	- a good mixture of sand and clay type soil	_____
28	TELRALA	- a fish uses this line to detect danger	_____
29	LNSE	- the eye uses this to focus light on the retina	_____
30	DIONIE	- added to salt it has prevented goitre	_____

The Numbers Game

The statements and the numbers have been mixed up. Can you sort them out? Put the correct number in the space provided.

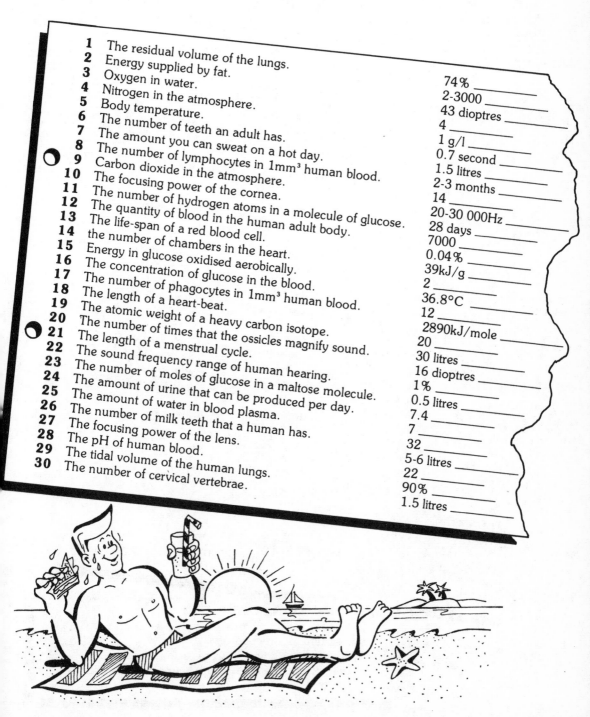

1 The residual volume of the lungs.
2 Energy supplied by fat.
3 Oxygen in water.
4 Nitrogen in the atmosphere.
5 Body temperature.
6 The number of teeth an adult has.
7 The amount you can sweat on a hot day.
8 The number of lymphocytes in 1mm³ human blood.
9 Carbon dioxide in the atmosphere.
10 The focusing power of the cornea.
11 The number of hydrogen atoms in a molecule of glucose.
12 The quantity of blood in the human adult body.
13 The life-span of a red blood cell.
14 the number of chambers in the heart.
15 Energy in glucose oxidised aerobically.
16 The concentration of glucose in the blood.
17 The number of phagocytes in 1mm³ human blood.
18 The length of a heart-beat.
19 The atomic weight of a heavy carbon isotope.
20 The number of times that the ossicles magnify sound.
21 The length of a menstrual cycle.
22 The sound frequency range of human hearing.
23 The number of moles of glucose in a maltose molecule.
24 The amount of urine that can be produced per day.
25 The amount of water in blood plasma.
26 The number of milk teeth that a human has.
27 The focusing power of the lens.
28 The pH of human blood.
29 The tidal volume of the human lungs.
30 The number of cervical vertebrae.

74% _____
2-3000 _____
43 dioptres _____
4 _____
1 g/l _____
0.7 second _____
1.5 litres _____
2-3 months _____
14 _____
20-30 000Hz _____
28 days _____
7000 _____
0.04% _____
39kJ/g _____
2 _____
36.8°C _____
12 _____
2890kJ/mole _____
20 _____
30 litres _____
16 dioptres _____
1% _____
0.5 litres _____
7.4 _____
7 _____
32 _____
5-6 litres _____
22 _____
90% _____
1.5 litres _____

The letters of each answer are jumbled up and one letter is missing. Fill in the missing letter. When read downwards they spell out the answers to the Extra Clues.

_ TIUECL — This waxy layer is common on evergreen leaves.

_ IELNC — The phylum produced by algae and fungi living together symbiotically.

_ ENHE — This loop's length affects the amount of water that is reabsorbed into the bloodstream by the kidneys.

_ OVRMINE — An animal which eats both plants and animals.

_ OCENA — The front part of the eye which plays a part in focusing light.

_ ECDULCD — The type of front produced when a warm front is overtaken by a cold one.

_ IIXNG — This type of bacteria lives in the root nodules of legumes, e.g. clover.

_ OWF — Electricity occurs when electrons do this.

_ MLPYH — The level of classification which occurs between kingdom and class, e.g. vertebrates.

_ GARISNSM — Living things are called this.

_ AETH — This type of muscle is myogenic. It does not need to be stimulated by the nervous system every time it contracts.

_ AECPTRL — These powerful muscles of a bird are attached to its keel.

_ EDAY — Milk is sometimes sterilised so that it does not do this so quickly.

_ ULJE — A unit of energy.

_ TAANGE — The secondary colour produced when red and blue are mixed.

_ PIUL — The eye hole whose size is controlled by movements of the iris.

_ UFETS — The embryo which develops inside the mother's uterus.

_ LAAXSE — The type of reproduction which involves only one organism.

_ ACAL — The ear one ends in the eardrum.

_ NAEIEN — The D.N.A. base which always pairs with thymine.

_ CEBPI — The antagonistic muscle pair to triceps.

_ ITL — Another name for the caudal fin of a fish.

_ RANISTT — The form of nitrogen that plants can absorb.

_ ABHE — The name of the industrial process in which ammonia is made.

_ BDAMEN — The other body segment of an insect. Head, thorax and

_ REOUVTI — This jelly-like humour lies between the lens and the retina, giving shape to the eye.

_ RLMA — Teeth with flattened surfaces used to crush food.

_ KMI — Fluid secreted by the mammary glands.

_ FICPCEI — Enzymes are this because they only act on one chemical.

VERTICAL EXTRA CLUES

1   These are causing the ozone layer of the atmosphere to be destroyed.   (6,6,9)

2   The answer to Vertical Clue 1 is being introduced into the atmosphere by use of these spray cans.   (8)

The Numbers Game

The statements and the numbers have
been mixed up. Can you sort them out?
Put the correct number, and unit if it
has one, in the space provided.

1 The neutral pH.
2 Oxygen boils at this temperature.
3 The % carbon in pig iron.
4 The number of oxygen atoms in one molecule of
   sodium sulphate.
5 The volume occupied by one mole of gas at S.T.P.
6 The temperature at which particles stop moving.
7 The height of a column of mercury one atmosphere of
   pressure can support.
8 Our body temperature.
9 The number of protons in $_{19}^{39}X$ where X is an
   element.
10 The uranium isotope used in nuclear reactors.
11 White phosphorus is converted to red phosphorus at this
    temperature.
12 The number of positive charges an aluminium ion has.
13 The temperature of superheated water used in the
    Frasch process.
14 The distance between the layers in graphite.
15 The number of hydrogen atoms in a molecule of propene.
16 The maximum number of electrons in an M shell or
    third energy level.
17 The heat of neutralisation of many acids and alkalis.
18 The percentage of N_2 in the air.
19 The number of elements known.
20 The number of neutrons in $_{20}^{60}X$ where X is an element.
21 The temperature at which diesel oil comes off from crude
    oil during fractional distillation.
22 The boiling point of ethanol.
23 Nitrogen boils at this temperature.
24 The number of hydrogen atoms in the compound called
    pentene.
25 The mass number of $_{19}^{39}X$ where X is an element.
26 An alkane with this number or more of carbon atoms
    per molecule is solid at room temperature.

78%
— 57 kJ/mole
7

40
250° Celsius
16

3
105

−273° Celsius
−183° Celsius

270° Celsius
760 mm

39
0.34 nm
18

4
78° Celsius
37° Celsius
6
4%

−196° Celsius
235
10

170° Celsius
24 dm^3

19

The Numbers Game

The statements and the numbers have been mixed. Can you sort them out? Put the correct number, and unit if it has one, in the space provided.

1 Rhombic sulphur is the allotrope form of sulphur below this temperature.

2 The most acidic pH.

3 The number of bonds between the carbon atoms in an ethyne molecule.

4 The mass of one mole of ammonium nitrate NH_4NO_3.

5 The relative atomic mass of calcium.

6 The number of coulombs of electricity that equal one faraday.

7 The number of protons most commonly found in an oxygen atom.

8 The temperature at which the Contact process is run.

9 The percentage of oxygen found in air.

10 The number of double bonds in an alkane.

11 The most alkaline pH.

12 The maximum number of electrons in the K shell, or first energy level of an atom.

13 Avogadro's constant — the number of atoms in a mole.

14 The number of coulombs produced if one amp flows for one second.

15 The maximum number of electrons in the L shell or second energy level of an atom.

16 The number associated with Newlands and his work on the periodic table.

17 The number of carbon atoms in a molecule of butane.

18 The temperature at which the destructive distillation of coal occurs.

19 The number of hydrogen atoms in a molecule of propane.

20 The temperature at which sulphur melts.

21 The boiling point of water.

22 The temperature at which graphite boils.

23 Above this temperature the bitumen fraction of crude oil can be collected.

24 The specific heat capacity of water in kJ/kg/°C.

25 An electron is this many times lighter than a proton or neutron.

26 When an isotope loses an α particle it loses this number of protons and neutrons.

_____ 8_

_____ 8

_____ 1000° Celsius

_____ 21%

_____ 14

_____ 6×10^{23}

_____ 373 K

_____ 119° Celsius

_____ 40

_____ 4.2

_____ 96° Celsius

_____ 16

_____ 8

_____ 96 500

_____ 4830° Celsius

_____ 1

_____ 2

_____ 8

_____ 350° Celsius

_____ 1840

_____ 2

_____ 450° Celsius

_____ 1

_____ 0

_____ 3

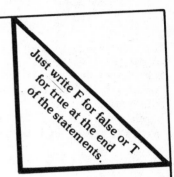

TRUE OR FALSE

Just write F for false or T for true at the end of the statements.

1   Solid sediment sinks to the bottom.
2   The alternative name for styrene is phenylethene.
3   Robert Brown is the scientist famous for discovering pollen grains.
4   The carbon dioxide molecule is trigonal in shape.
5   A trimer is a substance made from the combination of three molecules of a monomer.
6   Stainless steel is made of iron, carbon and chromium.
7   Ytterbium is the name of a transition element.
8   Hydrogen sulphide is a brown gas which smells of bad eggs.
9   A solid sublimes when it changes into a gas without melting.
10 According to the kinetic theory, particles in solids vibrate but do not move.
11 A spatula is used to move hot objects.
12 Calcium carbonate is very soluble in water.
13 Coal always burns with a smoky flame.
14 Large underground deposits of ammonia can be found in Texas.
15 In endothermic reactions the temperature of the surroundings increases.
16 Sulphite contains an SO_3^{2-} anion and is a salt of sulphurous acid.
17 Potassium chloride, otherwise known as saltpetre, is used to preserve meats.
18 An alpha particle is a fast-moving electron emitted from the nucleus of a radioactive atom.
19 Viscous describes a fluid which moves in a treacle-like manner.
20 Silicon dioxide occurs in many forms such as quartz and sand.
21 A very weak solution of potassium permanganate is pink.
22 Solar, wind and hydro-electric power are all renewable sources of energy.
23 Records are made from the nylon polymer.
24 Polyvinylchloride is made by condensation polymerisation.
25 Kineo, a Greek word, means particle — hence the name kinetic theory.

THE WHEEL

Answer each of the 20 clues and put each answer into the wheel, radially. (If you are not sure how to fill in the wheel, refer to Puzzle 3.) When completed, you will find the answers to the Outer Circle Clue around the outer circle, starting from 1. The inner circle will provide the letters to answer the Inner Circle Clues.

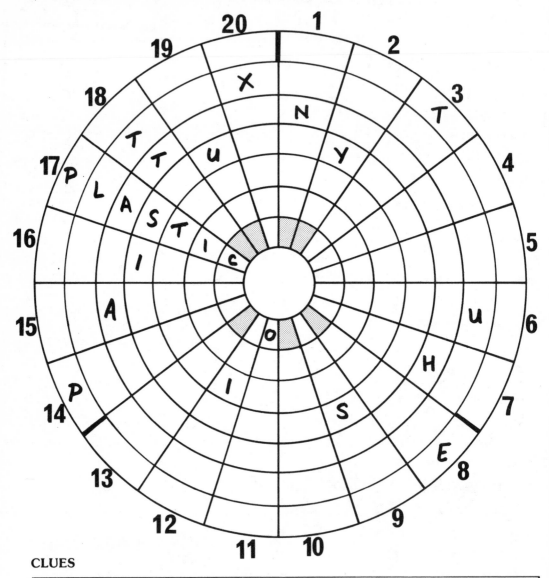

CLUES

1   Naturally occurring inorganic substance.

2   Biological catalysts, e.g. pepsin, amylase, trypsin.

3   Use of radioactivity which allows a process, e.g. photosynthesis, to be followed.

4   Around any ion in a metallic structure there are six other ions arranged in the shape of this.

5   This white solid, formula Al_2O_3, occurs normally as bauxite.

6   This type of fusion involves two nuclei combining to form a larger one.

MATERIALS AND THEIR PROPERTIES

CLUES

7 These fumes from a vehicle may contain poisonous lead compounds.
8 Latent heat is *this* when steam condenses to form water.
9 Generally, metals have a higher _____ strength than non-metals.
10 Chlorine and fluorine are members of this group in the periodic table.
11 The _____ chemical series is a list of elements in order of their electrode potentials.
12 This type of compound contains nitrogen and a reactive metal.
13 A substance which cannot be split into simpler substances by a chemical reaction.
14 In a _____ alcohol the carbon atom attached to the hydroxyl group has two hydrogen atoms attached to it.
15 A substance used to start a chemical reaction which is also one of the reactants.
16 A name used for the energy level in which electrons travel around the nucleus.
17 _____ sulphur is made by pouring hot liquid sulphur into cold water to cool it rapidly.
18 The element with atomic number 39.
19 Starch and rubber are examples of _____ polymers.
20 A liquid does this when it changes into a gas.

OUTER CIRCLE CLUES
The names of three organic compounds can be found. They contain, respectively, one, two and three carbon atoms and, in order, single, double and triple bonds.
(7,6,7)

INNER CIRCLE CLUES
By using any letters except those in the shaded sections in the inner circle, answer the following clues.

1 A common one is hydrochloric acid. (The same word is an answer for one of the numbered clues.) (7)
2 If an industrial process has to shut down it will probably prove to be this. (6)

THE WHEEL

Answer each of the 17 clues and put each answer into the
wheel, radially. (If you are not sure how to fill in the
wheel, refer to Puzzle 3.) When completed, you will find
the answers to the Outer Circle Clue around the outer
circle, starting from 1. The inner circle will provide the
letters to answer the Inner Circle Clues.

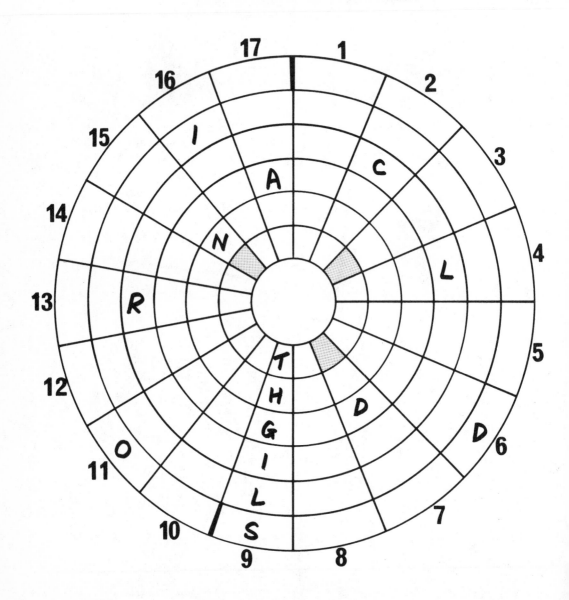

CLUES

1 The S.I. unit used to measure the strength of an electric current.
2 A _____ site occurs when an atom is missing from the crystal structure.
3 This gas supports combustion and dissolves in water to give a neutral solution.
4 Lead II sulphide is extracted from this ore.
5 This word describes any compound with the properties of an acid.
6 How we say $\triangle H$.
7 This word describes the movement of particles in a gas.
8 Sodium produces an _____-yellow colour in the flame test.
9 A word to describe the extent to which nitrogen dissolves in water.
10 The unstructured (amorphous) form of this element is called charcoal.
11 This alkane contains eight carbon atoms.
12 These are made from protons and neutrons.
13 Ionic bonding is _____ compared to covalent bonding.
14 The number of protons plus neutrons in a carbon atom.
15 Hydroxide, carbonate and sulphate are examples of these.
16 A commercial name for the widely used fertiliser ammonium nitrate.
17 Döbereiner suggested that elements be grouped in these.

OUTER CIRCLE RING: The number of particles per mole, equal to 6.02×10^{23} mol^{-1} is described as this. (9,8)

INNER CIRCLE RING: By using any letters except those in the shaded sections in the inner circle, answer the following clues.

INNER CIRCLE CLUES

1 A word to describe the electrons moving freely between metallic ions, to form metalic bonding. (3)
2 The number of electrons in an atom of oxygen. (5)
3 Powder which, after mixing with water, sets to a hard mass. Limestone and clay are used to make Portland _____. (6)

WORD BLOCKS

Answer the clues and fill in the horizontal lines of the grid. A word will be formed diagonally across the block, from top left. A clue is also given for this word.

A

1 The surname of the scientist who showed that the volume of a gas is directly proportional to its temperature (on the Kelvin scale) at a constant pressure.
2 If particles _____ more often, the rate of reaction increases.
3 Polymerisation involves monomers _____ with each other.
4 Nylon and P.V.C. are polymers which can be used to make some of the _____ we wear.
5 The enzyme present in saliva.
6 Substance formed when reactants react.
7 A flow of charged particles, either electrons or ions.

DIAGONAL
The industrial process which produces sulphuric acid.

Grid A (rows 1–7):
- Row 2: C
- Row 3: K ... G
- Row 6: P

B

1 The _____ of atomic shells is done by electrons.
2 Another word for combustion.
3 Sulphur trioxide is made by passing sulphur dioxide and oxygen over a heated catalyst, which can be this type of platinised wool.
4 Waste water from industry must be treated to remove pollution such as heavy metals and *this*.
5 This alkane, containing three carbons, is bottled and sold as a fuel for cooking and heating.
6 If the _____ area of the reactants is increased, the reaction will go faster.
7 This halogen gas dissolves in water to give an orange solution which is weakly acidic and acts as a bleach.

DIAGONAL
A blast _____ is used in the industrial production of iron.

Grid B (rows 1–7):
- Row 1: L ... G
- Row 4: Y
- Row 6: F
- Row 7: B

C

1 Chlorine gas can cause *this* by irritating the lungs.
2 This halogen is a dark-red fuming liquid at room temperature.
3 The atomic mass is always _____ than the atomic number.
4 Nitric acid is a highly corrosive acid which means that it _____ metals.
5 This inert gas has the symbol Kr and is used in some lasers.
6 The activation energy represents an energy _____ which must be overcome before a reaction can proceed.
7 Ions are electrically _____ particles.

DIAGONAL
Energy may be released but cannot be *this* during a chemical reaction.

D

1 In the Kellner-Solvay cell the cathode is a moving stream of mercury passing over *these*, which are made of carbon.
2 This burner is a common source of heat in the school laboratory.
3 This ion has more protons than electrons.
4 The first atomic energy level which can hold two electrons. (1,5).
5 Aliphatic organic compounds generally consist of these.
6 Describes a solution with a low concentration of solute.

DIAGONAL
The name of a four-carbon aliphatic compound containing one double bond.

E

1 The colour of universal indicator when the pH is above 11.
2 Hydrogen has the _____ number of protons compared with all other elements.
3 To change degrees Celsius to the _____ scale you must add on 273.
4 This sort of pump can be attached to a Buchner flask.
5 When sulphuric acid reacts with sodium chloride _____ hydrogen chloride fumes are produced.
6 The enzyme in yeast which can catalyse the conversion of glucose into ethanol.

DIAGONAL
This is 24 dm^3 for a mole of any gas measured at standard temperature and pressure.

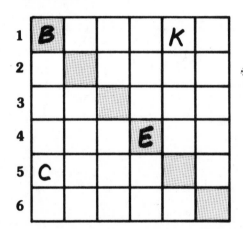

Find the answers to these clues in the word search grid. They may be in horizontal, vertical or diagonal lines, and letters may be used once, more than once, or not at all. The first letter and the number of letters in each answer are given in brackets after each clue to help you.

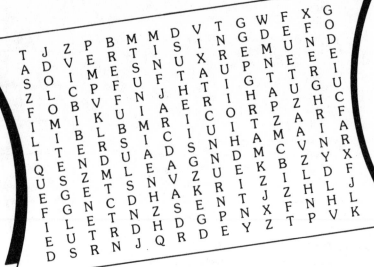

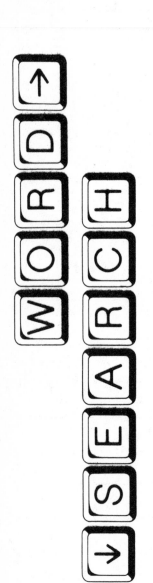

1 Neon is used in *these* signs and it emits a red glow when an electric discharge passes through it. (A) (11)
2 The destructive distillation of coal takes place at this number of degrees Celsius. (O,T) (3,8)
3 Substances used to destroy fungi, e.g. moulds and mildews which can damage crops. (F) (10)
4 Isotope of hydrogen with one proton and one neutron. (D) (9)
5 An _____ formula shows the simplest ratio of the atoms of each element contained in a compound. (E) (9)
6 Above the critical temperature, a gas cannot be *this* by pressure alone. (L) (9)
7 The process by which large alkanes are broken up into smaller alkanes and alkenes. (C) (8)
8 Magnesium occurs naturally as either magnesium chloride or in this rock, which is made of magnesium and calcium carbonate. (D) (8)
9 If malleable substances are _____ they can be formed into thin sheets. (H) (8)
10 In this aromatic compound the bonds between the six carbon atoms are midway in strength between a single and a double bond. (B) (7)
11 _____ law of diffusion states that the rate of diffusion of a gas is inversely proportional to the square root of its density. (G) (7)
12 The type of solution which limits pH changes when acids or alkalis are added to it. (B) (6)
13 The word missing from this statement — Absolute zero is equal to 273 degrees Celsius. (M) (5)
14 Describes a sample of a substance which has no detectable impurities. (P) (4)
15 The _____ of a reaction can be affected by temperature, pressure, concentration, surface area or a catalyst. (R) (4)
16 Aromatic compounds all have a closed _____ of six carbon atoms. (R) (4)

Find the answers to these clues in the word search grid. They may be in horizontal, vertical or diagonal lines. Letters may be used once, more than once, or not at all. The first letter and the number of letters in each answer are given in brackets after each clue.

Word Search

```
J N C K Y K R O C U V H Y U J
Y E O J D E S I N I T A L P N O
A L K I Q T P M H E G X G G O I
E B K N O R E M G K R N N N T
R I J O A I O T R N I E F I A
N C O M Z I N E E T Z H M G C
U S N F R S T C A C I U P G I
O I O Q P A G R G O I U U U O
D M I W I R I H E L A B E E S
T E T F S Z M C A Q R S R R S
S H A O A W L Z G F D Y S P I
U A R U R M J E A D E G Y E D
R E T L U Z R F G E G G D H Z
S V L B E Z R E P C U F U L I
Q U F L S U O N I U F T I B
```

1 An addition reaction in which hydrogen atoms are added to an unsaturated compound. (H) (13)

2 A type of reversible reaction in which a compound is divided into other compounds or elements. (D) (12)

3 The tube used to make radioactivity measurements. (G,M) (6,6)

4 _____ oil is made by distilling the residue from the primary distillation of crude oil in a vacuum. (L) (11)

5 Magnetic and electric fields cause the _____ of α and ß particles, but not γ rays. (D) (10)

6 A type of household coal. (B) (10)

7 A piece of glass equipment used for drying. (D) (10)

8 A process which separates residue from filtrate. (F) (10)

9 _____ ceramic wool is used as a catalyst in the production of sulphur trioxide. (P) (10)

10 The first power station to use a fast reactor for generating electricity was at this Scottish site. (D) (8)

11 Becquerel noticed this happened to the photographic plate he left in the dark under some uranium salt. (F) (7)

12 This alkene contains four carbon atoms and eight hydrogen atoms. (B) (6)

13 Describes two or more liquids which diffuse together. (M) (8)

14 Another name for this kind of sulphuric acid is oleum. (F) (6)

15 A lone _____ of electrons is donated by one atom to another in a dative covalent bond. (P) (4)

16 This common problem's other name is hydrated iron II oxide. (R) (4)

In each of the answers below the vowels have been given to you. The descriptions and answers are in the proper order. The groups of consonants at the bottom of the page provide the missing letters, one group being used for each answer.

All the Vowels

1 AE _ A _ E _	This type of concrete is lightweight because of the gas bubbles trapped in the mix.
2 _ A _ _ A _ E _ E	A reddish white metal, used in alloys such as special steels.
3 _ _ _ _ A _ I _ A _	The shape of the ammonia molecule.
4 _ A _ _ O _ A _ E _	One of the carbon compounds not included in organic chemistry.
5 _ E _ _ U _ I _	The name of a water softening process relying on ion exchange.
6 _ I _ A _ E _ _ _	Groups II and VI elements are this — having an electro valency of two.
7 _ I _ E _	_____ oxides behave as if they are mixtures of simpler oxides, e.g. red lead acts as a mixture of two parts lead II oxide and one part lead IV oxide.
8 _ _ O _ I _ E _	Compounds of bromine and one other element.
9 _ OI _ O _ OU _	One of the reasons a special method is needed to extract sulphur from the ground is the presence of _____ gas.
10 _ O _ _ E _ _ _ A _ E _	Describes a solution containing a lot of solute.
11 _ A _ I _ A _ _	Groups of atoms joined to make a negative ion, e.g. NO^{3-}
12 _ I _ _ I _ _ A _ E	In the distillation process a liquid _____ can be separated from a mixture of liquids and then collected.
13 _ _ O _ O _ _ _ _ O _ _ _ U E	This indicator is yellow below pH 6.5 and blue above pH 7.5. (11,5)
14 _ U _ _ _ A _ E	This compound contains an SO_4^{2-} and a cation.
15 _ E A _ A _ I _	This type of accumulator, used as a car battery, is a secondary cell.
16 _ A _ E _ _ _	The power of an ion to combine with another in an ionic bond is called its electro _____.
17 _ O _ _ A _ _	The reaction in which products are formed from original reactants in a reversible reaction is this, i.e. it goes from left to right.
18 _ A _ O _ I _ A _ IO _	The molar heat of _____ is the energy needed to change one mole of liquid into its gaseous form.
19 _ E _ O	– 273 Kelvin is absolute _____.
20 _ U _ _ _ IO _ A _	An atom or group of atoms that give a molecule its chemical properties is called its _____ group.

LETTERS TO BE USED

DSTLLT	FRWRD	PSNS	VLNCY	RTD	BRMTHYMLBL
VPRSTN	DVLNT	LD CD	PRMTT	RDCLS	CNCNTRTD
CRBNTS	FNCTNL	BRMDS	ZR	MXD	PYRMDL
SLPHT	MNGNS				

The words below are listed with their descriptions, but one letter is missing from each word. List the missing letters. When the letters are read downwards, they will spell out a very important law which applies to chemical reactions taking place in closed systems.

	Word	Description	Missing letter
____	DESICATOR	Hydrate salt may come out of this as an anhydrate.	____
____	FLURESCENT	Neon is used to give a red light in _____ discharge lamps.	____
____	DAIELL	This type of cell contains zinc and copper sulphate solutions.	____
____	CAUTIC SODA	A white deliquescent solid, otherwise called sodium hydroxide.	____
____	DISINFCTANTS	Some chlorine-containing compounds can kill germs and bacteria, therefore they are used in *these*.	____
____	FEMENTATION	Name given to the anaerobic respiration of yeast, which produces alcohol from sugar.	____
____	EAPORATES	A volatile liquid readily does this.	____
____	SPHALT	Bitumen plus mineral matter. Used in road-making.	____
____	DISILLATION	The liquid with the lowest boiling point will vaporise first during this process.	____
____	AMMONUM	This chloride sublimes on heating.	____
____	CLSED	A system in which no chemicals can enter or escape.	____
____	BALLOO	Often filled with helium, because it has a low density and is non-inflammable.	____
____	LEUM	Fuming sulphuric acid.	____
____	DIFRACTION	Crystals deflect X-rays to produce these patterns.	____
____	CALORIMTER	A bomb _____ is used to measure the heat of combustion of fuels.	____
____	FLIT	A form of silicon dioxide, not sand or quartz.	____
____	FISSIL	An element which can undergo fission is described as this.	____
____	BATTEY	This is an arrangement of two half cells of different elements.	____
____	RAHAM'S	_____ law states that the rate of diffusion of a gas is inversely proportional to the square root of its density.	____
____	CCLES	The name given to the circulations of nitrogen and of carbon through air, soil, animals and plants.	____

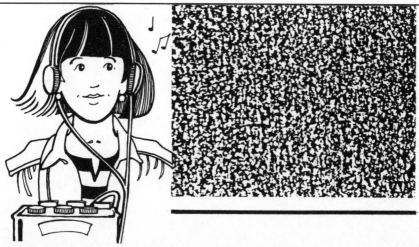

Missing Letter

The words below are listed with their descriptions, but one letter is missing from each word. When the letters are read downwards in each section, they will spell out words connected with the classification of elements. Clues are given for these words.

The vertical collections of similar elements in the periodic table.

▼

____ NEATIVELY	An anion is charged this way.	_____
____ BECQUEEL	A unit of radioactivity.	_____
____ METHYL-RANGE	This indicator is red below pH 3 and yellow above pH 4.5.	_____
____ GREENHOSE	The increasing levels of carbon dioxide in the atmosphere are increasing this effect.	_____
____ HASE	Water has a solid one, a liquid one and a gaseous one.	_____
____ MIT	A colloid consisting of tiny particles of a liquid dispersed in a gas.	_____

The horizontal collection of similar elements in the periodic table.

▼

____ PIETTE	Used to transfer definite small volumes of liquids.	_____
____ HOMOGNOUS	A catalyst in the same physical state as the reactants.	_____
____ AVOGADO	His hypothesis eventually led to the law named in his honour, that there are a constant number of particles in a mole of a substance.	_____
____ CHADWCK	The scientist who, in 1932, discovered neutrons.	_____
____ FAM	A colloid of small bubbles of gas in a liquid.	_____
____ SOLI	The state of matter in which particles have the least energy.	_____
____ J J THOMON	He first described the electron and showed that gases could conduct electricity.	_____

The scientist who thought elements could be grouped in threes or triads.

▼

____ TIAL	An alternative form of energy.	_____
____ MACRMOLECULE	A molecule containing a large number of atoms.	_____
____ LEACHING	This process removes colour from a material or solution. Most strong oxidising and redusing agents are also _____ agents.	_____
____ TAT	A type of pipette.	_____
____ LE CHATELIE	His principle states that if a change is made to a system in equilibrium the system itself will reduce the effect.	_____
____ STERIFICATION	An organic acid and alcohol partake in this type of reaction.	_____
____ HYDROPHILC	The part of a detergent molecule which is attracted to water.	_____
____ MONOCLIIC	This form of sulphur is more stable than rhombic above 96° Celsius.	_____
____ PHENOLPHTHALIN	This indicator is colourless below pH 8.5 and pink above pH 9.5.	_____
____ QUATZ	A form of silicon dioxide whose crystals find application in watches.	_____

Solve the clues and place your answers in their correct positions in the grid.

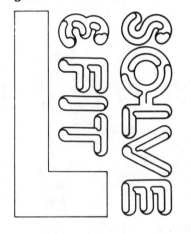

13-letter word
— This occurs when a nucleus disintegrates with a change in its atomic number.

11-letter word
— This word describes a liquid that does not evaporate easily. (3-8)

10-letter words
— Fine solid particles distributed in a liquid in which the solid does not dissolve are in _____.
— _ _ _ _ _ _ _ _ _ _ _ D is where most naturally occurring sulphur is found.

9-letter words
— The method of collecting a gas where the gas pushes water out from a gas jar placed on a beehive shelf. (4,5)

8-letter words
— Economically, industrial processes should not do this. (4,4)
— Another name for a teat pipette is a _____ pipette.
— A _____ usually consists of two or more atoms bonded together.
— Chlorine and oxygen _____ air, because they are heavier than air.
— Substances are chemically _____ if they are easily decomposed.
— The heavier particles of a solid, sinking to the bottom of a liquid, form *this*.

7-letter word
— A common name for acetic acid.

6-letter words
— This indicator is red below pH 7 and blue above it.
— This dicarboxylic acid's other name is ethanedioic acid.
— The molar _____ for any gas at standard temperature and pressure is 24 dm^3.

5-letter words
— A mixture, usually of metals, whose properties differ from those of the individual parts of the mixture.
— The number of electrons in the outer shell of a halogen gas.
— This has one less monomer than a trimer.
— _____ chloride polymerises to form a hard-wearing polymer, which is used to make records.
— Sulphur is used in many _____ which are essential to modern medicine.
— This liquid, made up of urea dissolved in water, is excreted from our bodies.

4-letter words
— _____ II chloride is an example of a ferrous compound.
— This bridge can be paper, soaked in potassium nitrate solution, and used to complete a circuit between two half cells.
— A cation has _____ electrons than the atom from which it was formed.
— An alternative energy source.

Solve the clues and place
your answers in their
correct positions in the
grid.

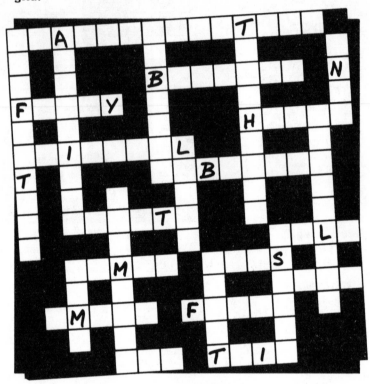

14-letter word
— There are three of these: solid, liquid and gas. (6,2,6)

10-letter word
— This type of substance lowers the surface tension of water.

9-letter words
— Materials which wear away the surface of another material.
— The study of the use of radioactive materials in medicine.
— There are millions of these in filter paper. (4,5)

8-letter words
— The temperature above which a gas cannot be liquified by pressure alone.
— When a radio-isotope, called a tracer, is introduced into a substance, the substance has been _____.
— There are over one hundred of these classified in the periodic table.

7-letter words
— The type of flask or funnel used when liquids are filtered using suction.
— The name given to the path which an electron takes around the nucleus of an atom.

6-letter words
— This third energy level can hold a maximum of eighteen electrons when full. (1,5)
— The substance which dissolves in a solvent to make a solution.

5-letter words

— A compound containing an -NH$_2$ functional group that is a weak base and has a characteristic fishy smell.

— Substances, sometimes called roughage, needed by many animals to help in the passage of food through the gut.

— Chemical plant needing supplies of water is often sited near rivers or _____.

— The layers in graphite are held together by weak forces, which explains the _____ state of graphite.

— _____ Becquerel was the discoverer of radioactivity.

— An example of a citrus fruit which contains citric acid.

— Hydrogen chloride forms steam fumes in _____ air.

4-letter words

— This nutritious drink is a colloid.

— A measurement of the amount of matter in a body.

— The hydrophobic hydrocarbon chain of a detergent molecule is sometimes called its _____.

— The trivial name for the calcium hydroxide which is added to acid soil to neutralise it.

— Tetraethyl lead is an _____-knock agent added to petrol.

— Density is this in solids when compared to liquids and gases.

3-letter word

— The number of carbon atoms in a benzene ring.

Answer the clues and put your answers in the grid. Some letters are entered already, to help you. Reading down the vertical lines of squares and circles will spell out other words, for which Extra Clues are given.

FIRSTS & SECONDS

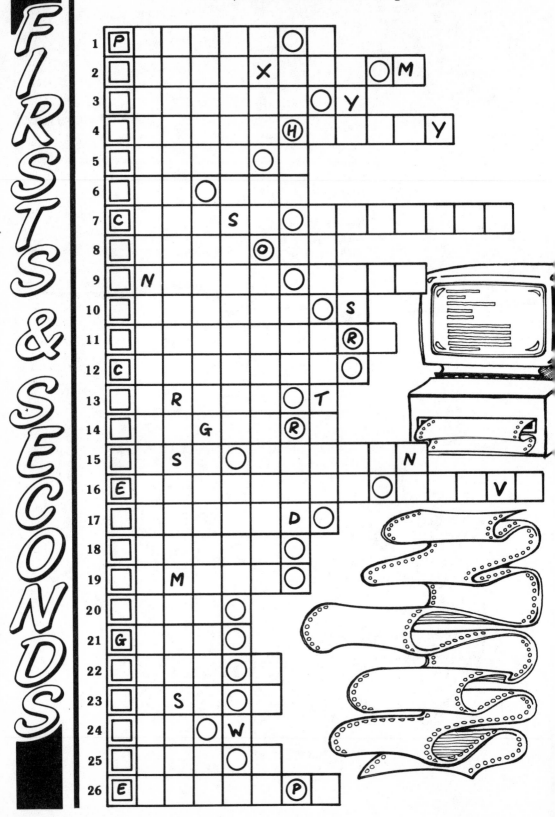

MATERIALS AND THEIR PROPERTIES

1 One factor which affects the rate of reaction. (8)
2 The name for the H_3O^+ion formed between H^+ ions and water when an acid dissolves in water. (11)
3 The number of atoms in a molecule, calculated from the molecular formula of the compound. (9)
4 Cancer can be treated by _____. (12)
5 Plastics can generally be _____ under the effects of heat and pressure. (7)
6 Protons in the nucleus _____ electrons orbiting the nucleus. (7)
7 The periodic table is an example of a _____. (14)
8 The name of a molecule containing one carbon and a (COOH) functional group. (8)
9 Any compound with a double or triple bond can be called *this*. (11)
10 Water covers just over this fraction of the Earth's surface. (3,6)
11 These change colour to mark the endpoint of a titration. (10)
12 The basic material of paper, found in plant cell walls. (9)
13 The light weight of aluminium makes its alloys an ideal building material for parts of these. (8)
14 Urea reacts very slowly with water to form ammonia compounds; it is, therefore, suitable as this kind of fertiliser. (4,4)
15 A slow combustion of glucose in animals, which produces energy. (11)
16 If *this* value is high, the atom will attract electrons to itself. (15)
17 A compound formed when chlorine reacts with another element. (8)
18 Gases collected by the upwards displacement of air must be _____ than air. (7)
19 This gas is dried by a rather unusual drying agent called quicklime, because it reacts with all the usual drying agents. (7)
20 This is formed by the radioactive decay of radium; its symbol is Rn. (5)
21 Substances with this type of atomic lattice are extremely strong and have very high melting and boiling points. (5)
22 This cannot be created or destroyed. (6)
23 A mixture of carbon monoxide and carbon dioxide would be passed through potassium hydroxide solution to remove the carbon dioxide, because potassium hydroxide will _____ carbon dioxide. (6)
24 The stable allotrope of sulphur is rhombic, _____ 96° Celsius. (5)
25 An indicator which can be used in the form of a liquid or paper. (6)
26 The amount of energy that a substance contains. (8)

Extra Clues for Vertical Words

☐ **1-14** Chemistry plays an important part in the _____ industry, which produces medicinal drugs. (14)
☐ **15-26** Secondary cells are *this*. (12)
○ **1-10** The scientist who was the first to split the atom. (10)
○ **11-21** A type of coolant which must be a volatile liquid. Freons are commonly used today.
○ **22-26** The name of a vertical family of elements, found in the periodic table. (5)

55

Answer the clues and put your answers in the grid. Some letters are entered already, to help you. Reading down the vertical lines of squares and circles will spell out other words for which Extra Clues are given.

FIRSTS & SECONDS

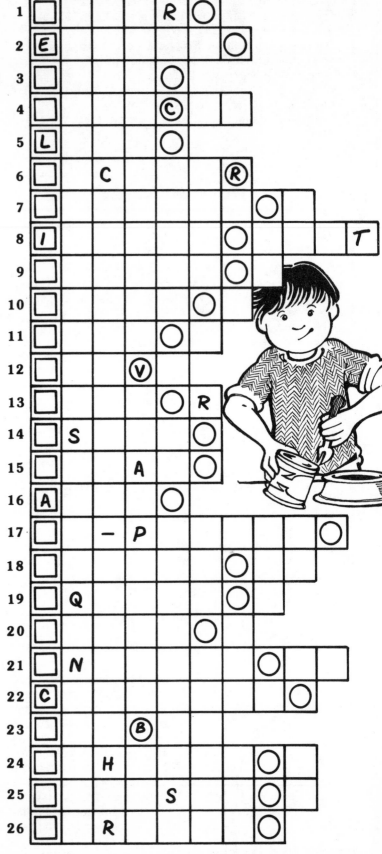

1 | | | | R | ○ |
2 | E | | | | | ○ |
3 | | | | | ○ |
4 | | | | ⓒ | |
5 | L | | | ○ |
6 | | | C | | | ⓡ |
7 | | | | | | ○ |
8 | I | | | | | ○ | | T |
9 | | | | | | ○ |
10 | | | | | ○ |
11 | | | | | ○ |
12 | | | ⓥ | |
13 | | | | ○ | R |
14 | | S | | | ○ |
15 | | | A | | ○ |
16 | A | | | ○ |
17 | | – | P | | | ○ |
18 | | | | ○ |
19 | Q | | | ○ |
20 | | | | ○ |
21 | N | | | ○ |
22 | C | | | | ○ |
23 | | | ⓑ |
24 | | H | | | ○ |
25 | | | S | | ○ |
26 | | R | | | ○ |

56

1   A natural fertiliser which can be spread on the soil to improve its nitrogen content. (6)
2   This is produced by the anaerobic fermentation of glucose by yeast. (7)
3   The number of electrons in the outer shell of a group III element. (5)
4   A substance which counteracts excess stomach acid by neutralising it. (7)
5   Lithium, beryllium and astatine are the _____ reactive members of their respective periodic table groups. (5)
6   The inside of a food can is covered in this, to give an unreactive layer between the can and its contents. (7)
7   This process involves losing electrons or hydrogen, or gaining oxygen. (9)
8   The rate of decay of a radioactive isotope is _____ of temperature. (11)
9   The reactivity of the elements will do *this* as you go down group VII in the periodic table. (8)
10 One way in which a detergent works is to lower the _____ tension of water. (7)
11 Particles in liquids are constantly in *this*. (6)
12 At any temperature _____ the transition temperature, monoclinic sulphur will be formed. (5)
13 The carbon dioxide molecule is an example of a *this* shaped molecule. (6)
14 The second atomic energy level, which can hold eight electrons when full. (1,5)
15 This alkane has two carbon atoms and thus, no isomers. (6)
16 The scientist who built the first mass spectrometer. (5)
17 Hydrogen is an example of an important *this*, when it is produced in the manufacture of sodium hydroxide by electrolysis. (2-7)
18 This phenomenon causes nitrogen and oxygen to react together to form nitrogen monoxide, which then forms soil nitrates. (9)
19 A useful summary of a chemical reaction. (8)
20 A form of carbon that appears as a transparent colourless crystal. (7)
21 Lithium is *this*, compared to francium. (10)
22 Cracking is a process which can be thermal or _____. (9)
23 This raw material, obtained from trees, is important in the industrial production of paper. (6)
24 A catalyst which slows down the rate of a reaction is called an _____. (9)
25 This type of rock is worn down because rain water contains dissolved carbon dioxide, which can react with it to form a slightly soluble compound. (9)
26 In an atomic bomb, the fission of _____ uranium−235 atoms happens in an uncontrolled manner. (8)

Extra Clues for Vertical Words

☐ 1-10 These elements cannot be described as metals or non-metals, although they have some of the properties of both. (10)

☐ 11-19 A word to describe substances which can be hammered into sheets. (9)

☐ 20-26 A word to describe substances which can be drawn out into wires. (7)

○ 1-9 Sub-atomic particles which occupy specific shells or energy levels. (9)

○ 10-17 This form of bond can be single, double, triple or dative. (8)

○ 18-26 The attraction of anions and cations is the basis of this type of attraction between atoms. (5,4)

Bits & Pieces

Answer the clues, using the groups of letters at the bottom of page
59 and fill in the grid, below. The letters may be used only once.
The number in the top corner of each box tells you to which answer
the group of letters belongs. Some letters have been put in the grid
to help you. When you have finished, two more words will be
revealed by reading down the first column. The groups of letters
which remain after all the clues have been answered will give a
phrase (3,5,2,14). This phrase is the clue to the two vertical words
(8) and (12).

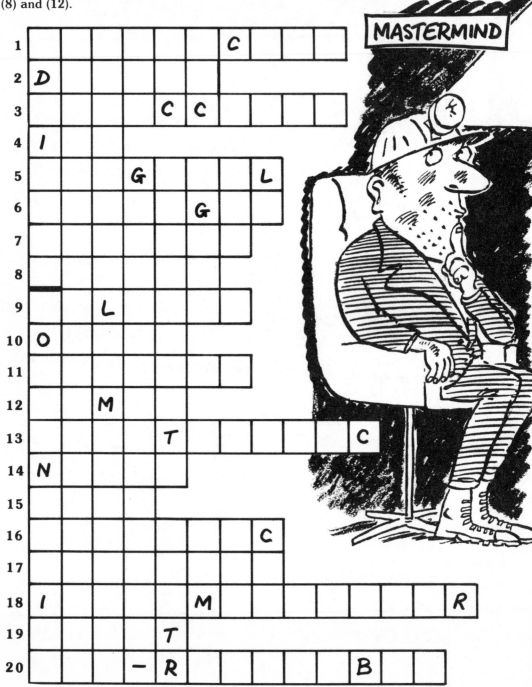

MASTERMIND

1 There are three forms of coal — lignite, bituminous and this. (10)

2 After centrifugation, you must _____ the liquid to separate it from the solid. (6)

3 Large, made of glass, this piece of laboratory equipment might contain a drying agent such as silica gel in order to do its job. (10)

4 Compounds ending in this contain two elements or radicals. (3)

5 Boron trichloride is an example of a molecule with a _____ planar shape. (8)

6 Its molecules have no volume, do not attract each other, they move in straight lines and they do not lose any energy when they collide. (5,3)

7 Nitric acid is made in this industrial process. (7)

8 This powerful oxidising agent, _____ acid, reacts with bases to give nitrate salts and water. (6)

9 A mixture of small particles dispersed in a solution. (7)

10 The number of electrons in this shell is the same as the element's group number. (5)

11 These swellings on the roots of leguminous plants, e.g. clover, contain nitrogen-fixing bacteria. (7)

12 A substance with molecules, formed from two monomer molecules. (5)

13 An _____ reaction produces a fall in the temperature of the system. (11)

14 A strong, hard-wearing member of a family called the polyamides. (5)

15 In a blast furnace this floats on top of the molten iron. (4)

16 These organic compounds contain a benzene ring. (8)

17 Transition metal, used to make lamp filaments, whose symbol is W. (8)

18 Weak attractive force, caused by uneven movement of electrons in the atoms of molecules, is an _____ force. (14)

19 An electron shell, with eight electrons contains an _____ of electrons. (5)

20 Some of the Earth's resources are this and are in danger of running out. (3-9)

20	17		7		3	1	7	2	11	10	13	3	18
NON	GS	TWO	OST	TY	OR	ANT	WA	DE	NOD	OUT	END	DES	IN
11	3	6		9		9		10	6	12	8	18	20
UL	IC	IDE	PES	ID	OF	COL	POL	ER	GAS	MER	NI	EC	RE
20	18	5	5	1	18		7	1	15	2	14	5	17
LE	MOL	GO	NAL	HRA	UL	YME	LD	TE	SL	CA	LON	TRI	TEN
19	8	13	13	4	3	8	12	16	14	16	9	18	20
OC	IC	OT	HER	IDE	CAT	TR	DI	MAT	NY	ARO	LO	AR	AB
20	18	1	6	13		11		17	16	15	2	19	
NEW	TER	CI	AL	RIS	MIC	AT	ES	ION	TUN	IC	AG	NT	TET

BITS AND PIECES

Answer the clues, using the groups of letters at the bottom of page **61** and fill in the grid, below. The letters may be used only once. The number in the top corner of each box tells you to which answer the group of letters belongs. Some letters have been put in the grid to help you. When you have finished, more words will be revealed. An Extra Clue is given for these words. The groups of letters remaining after all the clues have been answered will give more words, which are also clued.

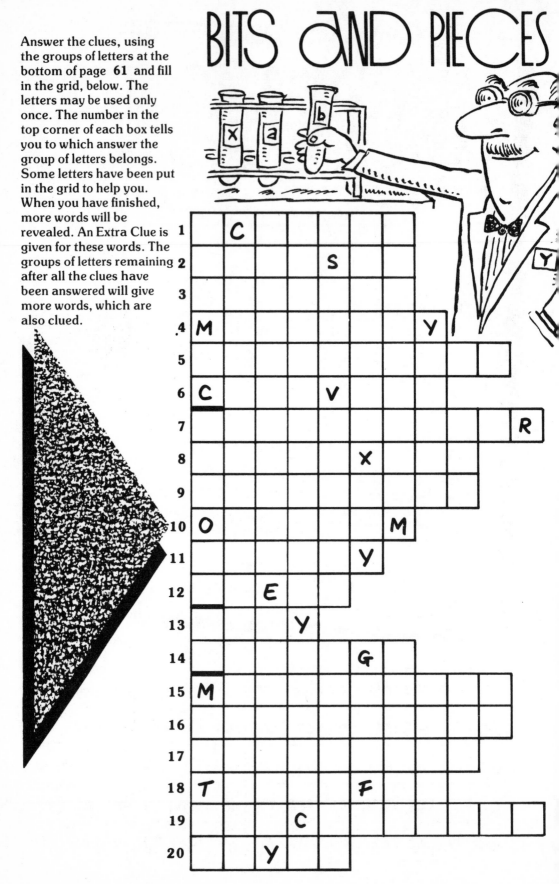

1   The other name for this compound is propanone. (7)
2   The scientist who discovered the electron. (7)
3   Branch of chemistry that studies all carbon compounds, except for carbonates and the oxides of carbon. (7)
4   A term used to describe the concentration in moles of solute per dm^3 of solution, also known as the M value. (8)
5   The process of forming ions. (10)
6   A plane of particles along which a crystal can be split. (8)
7   Instrument used to measure temperature. (11)
8   A compound made of a (OH) ion and a cation. (9)
9   A formula which does not give the total number of atoms in a covalent compound, but gives their ratio. (9)
10 Ion formed when a hydrogen ion attaches to a water molecule. (7)
11 The scientist who helped to discover and identify five of the noble gases. (6)
12 You can affect this aspect of a reaction by varying the pressure, concentration and temperature according to Le Chatelier's principle. (5)
13 Concentrated sulphuric acid is a colourless, _____ liquid. (4)
14 An atom of another element, which breaks up the regular crystalline structure, is described as this. (7)
15 Elements having either one or seven electrons in their outer shell. (10)
16 This is made up mostly of nitrogen. (10)
17 A volumetric analysis which involves adding one solution to another, using a burette. (9)
18 Ionic bonding involves the _____ of electrons between atoms. (8)
19 Graphite is the only non-metal able to conduct this. (11)
20 Sulphuric acid is important in the production of this artificial fibre used in clothing. (5)

Extra Clue for Vertical Words
Published in 1808, this attempts to explain how atoms behave. (6,6,2,6)

Remaining Letters Clue
The scientist responsible for the Vertical words is ___ ___ ___ ___ ___   ___ ___ ___ ___ ___ ___.

5	1	6	7	10	2	11	15	19
O ION	ACE	CLE	THE	NI	THO	SAY	NO	RIC
2	**6**	**13**	**8**	**7**	**14**	**8**	**16**	**15**
N AGE	OI	XI	HN	RMO	FOR	DRO	AT	VAL
1	**3**	**4**		**4**	**2**	**3**	**4**	**18**
O IC	MO	DAL	LA	MS	GAN	OR	RI	SF
7	**9**	**7**	**8**	**11**	**1**	**14**	**12**	**15**	**19**
R CAL	MET	DE	RAM	NE	GN	YI	ENT	CT
4	**5**	**17**	**6**	**8**	**13**		**17**	**18**	**18**
Y IS	ION	AV	HY	LY	TON	AT	TR	ER
10	**14**	**9**	**17**	**12**	**15**	**10**	**9**	**16**	**20**
XO EI	IRI	TI	ELD	MO	UM	EMP	MOS	ON
16	**19**	**5**	**18**	**5**	**16**	**17**	**19**	**20**
RE ELE	AT	AN	ION	PH	TR	ITY	RAY	

Complete the crossword in the normal way. However, your answers must be written with two or three letters in each square. Any single letters have been given. One answer and some double and treble letters have also been filled in to start you off. Hyphens are to be omitted, when filling in the grid.

CLUES ACROSS

1　These acidic substances are used to treat nettle and wasp stings which contain bases. (14)
3　The compound which combines with and carries oxygen around the blood. (11)
9　The sharing of electrons by all atoms in a molecule or giant metallic lattice. (14)
10　The second most common element in the Earth's crust, found in sand. (7)
11　*This* field can deflect α and β radioactive radiation. (8)
13　A soft, silver-white alkaline earth metal, used in fireworks. (9)
15　This smokeless fuel is made by heating coal in the absence of air. (4)
16　_____ blood can be added to soil with a low nitrogen content. (5)
17　_____ compounds contain Fe^{3+} ions. (6)
18　Such reactions have a positive heat of reaction, i.e. $\triangle H = +$. (11)
20　A series of organic compounds which increase in size by the addition of a (CH_2) group is _____. (10)

27 This type of molecule has no difference in charge at its ends. (3-5)
29 An acid is a substance that contains _____ hydrogen. (11)
30 When *this* is destructively distilled, ammonia, coal tar, coal gas and many other useful products are formed. (4)
31 This non-metallic group V member has a red and a white form; its ore is called apatite. (10)
33 A mixture of gases which surrounds the Earth. (3)
34 The amount of heat generated when one mole of a substance is completely burnt. (4,2,10)
35 Ionic, covalent and metallic are the three main types of *this*. (7)
37 _____ distillation is done by heating coal in the absence of air. (11)
38 Limestone reacts with rain-water to form this slightly soluble compound. (7,8,9)

CLUES DOWN

1 The thick layer of oxide put on aluminium in *this* process can be dyed to give aluminium an attractive finish. (9)
2 The site of the first nuclear bomb explosion in Japan. (9)
4 The _____ of γ rays does not change the number of protons or neutrons in an isotope. (8)
5 A state of America, rich in sulphur deposits. (9)
6 A flaw in a crystal structure, which involves the displacement of a row of atoms. (11)
7 The most common noble gas. (5)
8 A catalyst that is in a different physical state from the reactants. (May also be spelt _ _ _ _ _ _ _ _ E _ _ _.) (12)
12 The non-polar chain part of a detergent is called *this* because it is repelled by water. (11)
13 A triple bond has more _____ than a double bond, which has more than a single bond. (8)
14 Orlon, Courtelle and P.V.C. are examples of polymers which can be used to make _____. (6)
15 A combination of air and water are *this* to iron. (9)
19 A spherical grouping of detergent molecules in water. (7)
22 The occurrence of two or more different crystals of the same substance. (12)
23 Changes in *this* can be used to monitor the progress of reactions. (6)
24 Iron compounds containing Fe^{2+} ions are _____. (7)
25 This formula shows the three-dimensional arrangement of the atoms and bonds in a molecule. (14)
26 There is more _____ between the particles of a gas than those of a solid. (5)
27 Another name for inert gas. (5)
28 Such an element is not completely metal or non-metal, e.g. silica or boron. (9)
32 Industrial processes often operate at lower temperatures in order to keep *this* down. (4)
36 A _____ covalent bond can be called a co-ordinate bond. (6)
37 The rate of _____ of a radioactive substance is expressed in terms of its half-life. (5)

Complete the crossword in the normal way. However, your answers must be written with two or three letters in each square. Any single letters have been given. One answer and some double and treble letters have also been filled in to start you off. Hyphens are to be omitted, when filling in the grid. Note that the Clues continue on page 66.

CLUES ACROSS

1 Substances which form a concentrated solution on being exposed to the air are *this*, e.g. calcium chloride. (12)

3 Two or more liquids that do not diffuse together are called *this*. (10)

6 This is formed when a solid sublimes. (6)

8 A major area for the applications of chemistry is _____, where new fertilisers, weed- and pest-killers, for example, are in much demand. (11)

10 This noble gas is used in balloons and airships because, although denser than hydrogen, it is not inflammable. (6)

13 Words used in connection with this common compound include polar, solvent, hard and soft. (5)

14 Coating with zinc makes an iron object *this* to rusting. (9)

15 The individual molecule which goes to make up a polymer. (7)

17 A word to describe the smell of chlorine and hydrogen sulphide gas. (7)

21 This word describes how full the outer electron shell of a group IV element is. (4)

22 The crystals of the monoclinic form of sulphur are _____-shaped. (6)

23 Oxygen is colourless, odourless and _____. (9)

25 These "mites" are made of calcium carbonate. (6)

26 When solid fuels burn they leave *this* air pollutant, which contains solid metal oxides called basic oxides. (3)

27 This metal is a liquid at room temperature. (7)

29 Potassium's flame test colour. (5)

31 This ore, zinc _____, is also called zinc sulphide. (6)

33 A molecule with the same atoms as another molecule, but in different arrangement is called an _____. (6)

34 Galena is the name of *this* metal's most common ore. (4)

35 A metal consists of this type of regular arrangement of positive ions. (5-7)

39 A method of water-softening, involving zeolite, is based upon this. (3-8)

41 With the exception of those of Group I, these compounds are all insoluble in water, decompose on heating and give off carbon dioxide when they react with acids. (10)

43 A word used to describe the arrangement of positive ions found in metals. (7)

44 A molecule's _____ increases on heating. (5)

45 The removal of water from a substance is a _____ reaction. (11)

46 The presence of small amounts of carbon has a _____ effect on the iron alloy called steel. (9)

CLUES DOWN

1 In a cell or battery this is the amount of energy that is converted to electricity (the remainder is wasted). (5,1)

2 The process of separating different substances in a liquid which involves spinning the solution at high speed. (12)

3 If water is *this* it will not boil at 100° Celsius or freeze at 0° Celsius. (6)

4 Produced when soap is used in hard water. (4)

5 Mineral salts can be _____ out of a sandy soil. (7)

6 A _____ pump can be used to create suction which can be used when filtering with a Buchner funnel and flask. (6)

7 Radioactive fission of the 235 isotope of this element is used by nuclear power stations to provide energy. (7)

9 Hot air comes from *these* in the extraction of iron from its ore. (7)

11 In graphite one _____ is held to the next by Van der Waals' bonds. (5)

12 The least reactive halogen gas. (8)

13 Crystals which contain *this* are hydrated. (5,2,15)

16 Oxygen, hydrogen and nitrogen are all colourless, _____ and tasteless. (9)

17 The colour of a potassium permanganate solution. (6)

see over

18 The amount of energy that a substance contains which is impossible to measure directly. (8)

19 Universal indicator is this colour above pH 10. (6)

20 _____ liquor is one of the main products formed from the destructive distillation of coal. (10)

24 Fibrous silicate minerals, once used for fire-proofing but now considered a health-hazard. (8)

27 He arranged the elements in order of their relative atomic mass in the periodic table. (9)

28 Marie _____ discovered radium. (5)

30 The colour of molten sulphur. (5)

32 Graphite is described as a _____-coloured, opaque, shiny solid. (5)

36 All chemical equations should be _this_. (8)

37 This process makes rubber harder by reaction with sulphur. (11)

38 A covalent bond involves elements _____ with electrons. (7)

40 Raising the temperature gets particles into _this_ state. (7)

42 This chemical, used in agriculture, is part of the gasoline fraction produced in the primary distillation of petroleum. (7)

43 _These_ agents are electron donators or oxygen acceptors, e.g. carbon. (8)

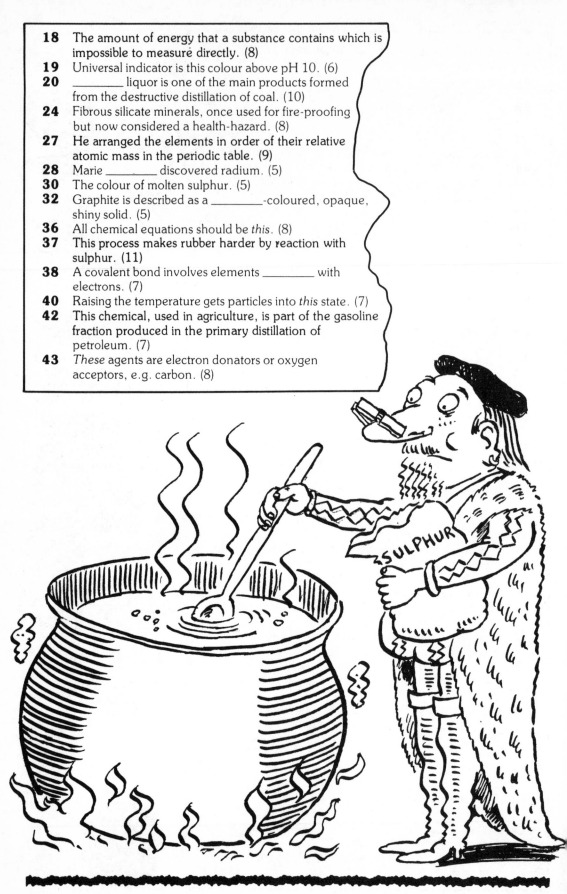

Below are anagrams of words, but each has one
letter missing. A clue is given to each word, and
in the proper order. List the missing letters.
When the letters are read downwards they spell
words which are also to do with apparatus.
Extra Clues are given for these words.

Missing Letter

1___MUE — Clues 1 and 4 — a glass-fronted cabinet containing an extractor fan. (4,8) _____

2___EABEK — Used to hold liquids — shows approximate volume. _____

3___VPAERTOING — An _____ basin is used to hold a solution when the solvent is being driven off using heat. _____

4___APBUORD — See 1. _____

5___ORIPD — Three legs, gauze goes on top, burner underneath. _____

6___EENVTRD — A funnel is *this* when hydrogen chloride is dissolved in water, to prevent water being sucked back into the apparatus. _____

7___SSAMCLPB — Holds glassware in position on a retort stand. (4,5) _____

8___OADE — The positive electrode. _____

9___LTPINUM — A type of wire that can be used in a flame test. _____

10___REBUTE — Used in titrations to dispense accurate volumes of liquid. _____

11___EVHEEB — Used to support a gas jar during gas collection by displacement of water. _____

12___FNUEL — A separating *this* is used to separate immiscible liquids. _____

13___EUAZ — Used to spread the heat of a bunsen burner evenly. _____

14___NTFERIUGE — Used to spin test tubes at high speed. _____

15___NIIIGTN — A tube in which small quantities can be melted or boiled. _____

16___UNFNE — A Buchner *this* is used when liquids are filtered with suction. _____

17___GBN — Placed in the end of a test tube, made of cork or rubber. _____

18___ASUNEIGR — Clues 18 and 21 — used to measure the approximate volume of liquids. (9,8) _____

19___AOICCL — Clues 19 and 20 — used in preference to a beaker when the container needs to be stoppered. (7,5) _____

20___SKLA — See 19. _____

21___NDYLECR — See 18. _____

22___IVEERDY — A tube used to carry gases. _____

23___ADCHOE — The negative electrode. _____

24___LUTVMORIC — A flask allowing accurate measurement of volume. _____

25___YIGSNE — A gas _____ can be used to receive gas from, or inject gas into, a reaction vessel. _____

26___ETIPTE — A teat _____ can dispense drops of liquid. _____

27___PT — Type of funnel which can dispense drops of liquid. _____

28___MUP — A vacuum _____ can be attached to a Buchner flask. _____

29___LISTHT — The type of funnel used to add a liquid to a reaction mixture. _____

30___TREOT — Stand used to hold apparatus in position. _____

Extra Clues for Vertical Words
1-19 Used to carry out fractional distillation of crude oil on an industrial scale.(13,6)
20-30 This is placed inside a filter funnel. (6,5)

The Numbers Game

The statements and the answers have been mixed up. Can you sort them out? Put the correct statement letter under each answer number in the grid below.

1	2	3	4	5	6	7	8	9	10	11	12	13	14	15

16	17	18	19	20	21	22	23	24	25	26	27	28	29	30

PHYSICAL PROCESSES

1	0 K	A	Density of water at 4°C
2	−39°C	B	Refractive index of water
3	9.81 m/s²	C	Latent heat of vaporisation of water
4	300 000 000 m/s	D	Absolute zero (Kelvin)
5	50 Hz	E	Atomic number of uranium
6	760 mm Hg	F	Refractive index of glass (air — glass)
7	1.0 g/cm³	G	Temperature at which water has its maximum density
8	−273°C	H	Boiling point of water (Celsius)
9	4°C	I	Freezing point of mercury
10	1.33	J	Density of meths in kg/m³
11	92	K	Approximate atmospheric pressure
12	4200 J/kg	L	Absolute zero (Celsius)
13	13 600 kg/m³	M	Acceleration due to gravity
14	800	N	Speed of light in vacuo
15	100 000 Pa	O	Density of mercury
16	0°C	P	Melting point of pure ice (Celsius)
17	37°C	Q	Frequency of A.C. mains
18	336 000 J/kg	R	Body temperature
19	42°	S	Latent heat of fusion of ice
20	330 m/s	T	Specific heat capacity of water
21	256 Hz	U	Height of column of mercury supported by atmospheric pressure
22	273 K	V	Root Mean Square value of mains voltage
23	240 V	W	Critical angle for glass
24	1.5 V	X	Speed of sound in air
25	12	Y	Frequency of tuning fork labelled C
26	100°C	Z	Melting point of pure ice (Absolute)
27	0.67	AA	Approximate voltage of a single cell
28	1.5	BB	Mass number of a normal carbon atom
29	373 K	CC	Refractive index of glass (glass — air)
30	2 260 000 J/kg	DD	Boiling point of water (Kelvin)

Solve the clues and place your answers in their correct positions in the grid. A few letters have been put into the grid to start you off.

12-LETTER CLUE
— This law of momentum states that the total momentum before collision is equal to the total momentum after collision.

11-LETTER CLUE
— Most solids have *this* structure.

10-LETTER CLUES
— *These* of molecules against the walls of a container create pressure.
— The ratio of voltage to current.

9-LETTER CLUES
— Putty is *this* because it does not return to its original size and shape.
— This new convention for solving mirror problems by calculation has distances measured in the direction of the incident light as positive.
— When the space above a liquid can hold no more vapour it is said to be *this*.

8-LETTER CLUE
— *This* combustion engine uses petrol as its fuel.

7-LETTER CLUES
— When 1 ampere flows for 1 second one of this quantity of electricity passes.
— Mass per unit volume.

6-LETTER CLUES
— The 240 V mains is the root mean _____ value of the voltage.
— Resistance is defined as the ratio of the potential difference _____ a conductor to the current flowing through it.
— A force which equals pressure × area.
— The diameter of this increases as the external pressure on it gets less.
— A metal to be found in a rechargeable cell along with cadmium.
— This type of tank is used to show waves in water.

5-LETTER CLUES
— *This* allows a current to flow through it in one direction only.
— *These* waves are longitudinal waves which will not pass through a vacuum.
— A frequency of one cycle per second is equal to one _____.

4-LETTER CLUES
— Units of atmospheric pressure.
— An electron _____ can be deflected by electric or magnetic fields.
— This radioactive particle is an electron.

3-LETTER CLUE
— A copper ion has this number of positive charges.

SCIENTISTS
A Mix Up

The names of these famous scientists and their discoveries have been mixed up. Can you match up the Name numbers with the correct Clue letters? Enter your answers in the grid below.

1	2	3	4	5	6	7	8	9	10	11	12	13	14	15

16	17	18	19	20	21	22	23	24	25	26	27	28	29	30

Name

1 Sir Humphry Davy
2 Robert Boyle
3 Wilhelm von Röntgen
4 Lord Kelvin

5 Christian Huygens

6 Otto von Guericke

7 Blaise Pascal

8 Willebrord Snell

9 Heinrich Hertz

10 Charles de Coulomb
11 Galileo Galilei
12 Michael Faraday
13 Anders Celsius

14 Sir J J Thomson

15 James Joule
16 Evangelista Torricelli

17 André Ampère

18 Sir Isaac Newton

Clue

A Devised a thermodynamic temperature scale.
B Put forward the wave theory of light.
C Invented the first barometer.
D Produced electricity from a pile of silver and zinc discs separated by cardboard soaked in brine.
E Investigated elasticity and the relationship between deformation and stress.
F Investigated the relationship between current and potential difference.
G Showed that mechanical and electrical energy could be transformed into internal energy.
H Investigated the relationship between the volume of a gas and its temperature.
I Showed that the mass of a body is a measure of the energy it contains.
J Invented the vacuum flask.
K Discovered the magnetic effect of a current.
L Invented the miner's safety lamp.
M Showed that during electrolysis the mass deposited is proportional to the quantity of electricity.
N Invented the air pump to show the effect of removing air from two hemispheres.
O Discovered thermionic emission.
P Discovered that pressure is transmitted equally through a fluid.
Q First compared the radiating powers of different surfaces.
R Investigated the relationship between pressure and volume of a gas.

19	John Leslie	**S**	Carried out experiments on the mass and charge of electrons.
20	Archimedes	**T**	Showed that charge always remains on the outside surfaces of a conductor.
21	Alessandro Volta	**U**	Showed that the molecules of liquids and gases are continually moving.
22	Sir James Dewar	**V**	Discovered polonium.
23	Hans Christian Oersted	**W**	Dropped three balls of different masses from the Leaning Tower of Pisa and found they reached the ground simultaneously.
24	Jacques Charles	**X**	Showed electromagnetic waves could be produced from an oscillating spark.
25	Robert Brown	**Y**	Discovered X-rays.
26	Albert Einstein	**Z**	First used a solenoid for magnetising steel needles.
27	Marie Curie	**AA**	Showed that a gravitational force exists between all bodies.
28	Thomas Edison	**BB**	Suggested dividing the temperature scale into 100 divisions.
29	Georg Ohm	**CC**	Showed that the upthrust of a liquid on a body equals the weight of fluid displaced.
30	Robert Hooke	**DD**	Discovered the relationship between the angles of incidence and refraction.

Bits & Pieces

Answer clues 1-25, using the groups of letters provided in the boxes on page **75**. Each group may be used only once. The number in each box tells you to which answer the group of letters belongs, e.g. SPL in the first box belongs to Answer 1. When you have finished, three more words will be revealed by reading down the first vertical column. An Extra Clue is given for these. The unused groups of letters will spell out a description of the vertical words.

1 SPL	8 TH	2 ALT	3 ION	4 EYE	1 RI	9 CO	7 IN	9 ROG	15 AX	12 LO	18 COM	2 OR	20 NS	21 OSC
3 THE	7 RD	3 RM	2 NAT	3 IC	18 OR	9 ELE	9 CT	6 LAT	15 ALL	16 TRA	18 MUT	19 AMP	22 RES	23 BI
8 ERM	11 EBO	2 ER	1 IT	10 SEC	4 PIE	10 ON	14 NI	5 LIN	13 LA	17 UL	19 LI	19 TU	22 OL	21 ATE
16 NS	10 DA	1 NG	8 AL	11 NI	5 EAR	17 INS	6 ENT	12 SS	15 PAR	18 AT	17 OR	17 AT	23 CON	22 UT
9 PE	16 MER	14 IO	7 WA	10 RY	14 SED	13 MP	4 CE	11 TE	16 FOR	19 DE	20 LE	21 ILL	24 ION	22 ION
25 RA	24 OV	23 ERE	25 AL	24 CA	23 TEM	24 OS	VE	PH	IN	25 SHA	25 RY	25 PO	PE	

CLUES

1 This type of commutator is found on a D.C. motor. (5,4)

2 In a car this provides the electrical energy. (10)

3 In this type of emission electrons leave a hot filament. (10)

4 In optical instruments this is the lens you look through. (8)

5 This type of expansion measures the increase in length. (6)

6 This type of heat is hidden. (6)

7 Forces in a water drop act in an _____ direction. (6)

8 A current of warm rising air which can be used by a glider. (7)

9 A device for detecting electrostatic charges. (12)

10 The output coil of a transformer. (9)

11 A material that when rubbed with fur gives a negative charge. (7)

12 In a thermos flask, heat _____ by conduction from a hot liquid is reduced by having a vacuum between the glass walls. (4)

13 A component which converts electrical energy into light energy. (4)

14 When a charged particle passes through the window of a Geiger tube some of the gas inside is *this*. (7)

15 This is a method of locating exact positions of images in mirrors or lenses. (8)

16 A device for stepping up and stepping down voltages. (11)

17 A material which does not conduct electricity. (9)

18 A split-ring *this* carries the induced current from the coil of a D.C. dynamo. (10)

19 The maximum displacement from the mean position during oscillation. (9)

20 An optical instrument used in a magnifying glass. (4)

21 A column of air can be made to do this if a tuning fork is held above it. (9)

22 *This* of forces gives the magnitude of a force in a given direction. (10)

23 A type of lens with two inwardly curving surfaces. (9)

24 This layer of the Earth's atmosphere reflects radio waves. (10)

25 Soft iron forms this type of magnet. (9)

Extra Clues

Vertical words
The three vertical words form a phrase describing a space station's path around the planet Earth. (10,10,5)

Remaining letters
Three words describing the vertical words. (4,2,5)

FIRSTS & SECONDS

Answer the clues. Reading downwards, from top to bottom, the squares and circles will reveal more words. There are Extra Clues for these words. A few letters have been put into the grid, to help you.

CLUES

1. The _____ expansivity is the fractional increase in length per kelvin increase in temperature.
2. This pressure is measured by a barometer.
3. This for a rocket depends on the law of conservation of momentum.
4. The loss of power by the energy being being absorbed.
5. Two colours which give white light when mixed are this.
6. Another name for the angle of dip.
7. This is used with a special timer to show the distance moved by an object every one-fiftieth of a second. (6-4)
8. The principal one for a spherical mirror is the line joining the pole of the mirror to its centre of curvature.
9. The mass *this* of an element is the number of protons and neutrons in the nucleus.
10. The radius of *this* is twice the focal length of a spherical mirror.
11. When this moves between the Sun and the Moon a lunar eclipse occurs.
12. A _____ device has a scale marked on it.
13. One flows when the rate of charge past a point is 6×10^{18} electrons per second.
14. A metal used to absorb gamma radiation.
15. When air is made to do this sound waves are produced.
16. Rate of change of velocity.
17. This pole of a magnet always points to magnetic north when freely suspended. (5-8)

18. A hydraulic jack is a machine which is _____. (3-6)
19. This advantage is the ratio of the load and effort.
20. This type of energy is produced by rotating a coil of wire in a magnetic field.
21. The study of heat and energy.
22. Swan did his work on the filament lamp in this country.
23. A glass block whose section is a _____ is used to demonstrate refraction of light.

Extra Clues

☐   1-11   Charge divided by potential.
☐   12-23   A sensitive current-measuring device.
○   1-4   The mica window of a Geiger Müller tube must be *this* to allow alpha particles through.
○   5-13   An instrument which measures height by the vertical change in air pressure.
○   14-23   *These* isotopes are man-made.

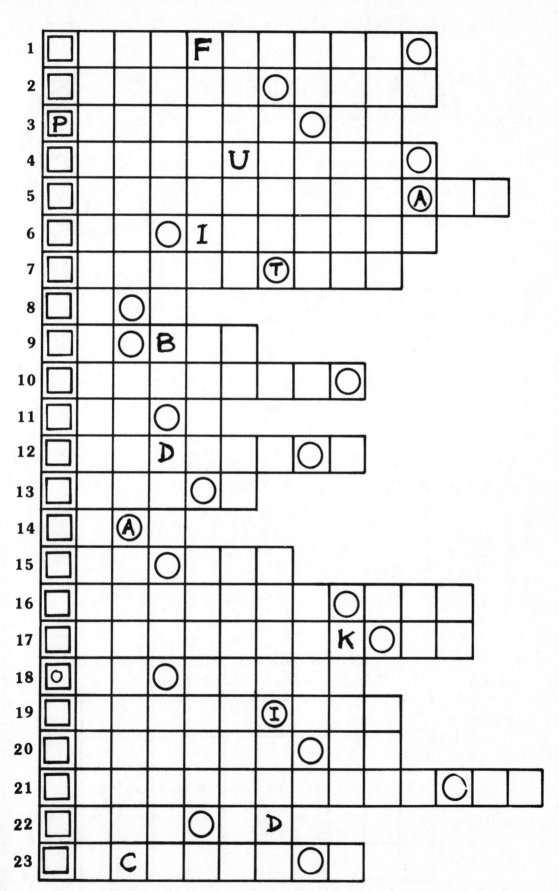

UNITS AND PREFIXES

A MIX UP

The symbols, units or prefixes, and their descriptions, have all been confused. Can you sort them out? Enter your answer in the grid provided. One answer has been entered to start you off.

SYMBOL		UNIT/PREFIX		DESCRIPTION	
1	m	A	Micro	AA	Unit of potential difference
2	k	B	Volt	BB	Unit of temperature (Celsius)
3	m	C	Ohm	CC	Unit of resistance
4	μ	D	Metre	DD	One thousand of the base unit
5	M	E	Degree	EE	1 J/s
6	n	F	Second	FF	Unit of energy
7	G	G	Degree Celsius	GG	Unit of charge
8	kg	H	Kilo	HH	Basic unit of length
9	L	I	Watt	II	Unit of frequency
10	s	J	Joule	JJ	Unit of current
11	Hz	K	Mega	KK	One millionth of the base unit
12	N	L	Hertz	LL	Unit of mass
13	J	M	Kilogram	MM	Unit of an angle
14	W	N	milli	NN	1/1000 of the base unit
15	Pa	O	Pascal	OO	Unit of force
16	°C	P	nano	PP	10^{-9} times base unit
17	K	Q	Litre	QQ	Absolute unit of temperature
18	°	R	Kelvin	RR	10^9 times base unit
19	F	S	Giga	SS	1 N/m²
20	C	T	Farad	TT	One million
21	V	U	Newton	UU	Unit of liquid volume
22	A	V	Coulomb	VV	Unit of capacitance
23	Ω	W	Ampere	WW	Unit of time

number	1	2	3	4	5	6	7	8	9	10	11	12
unit/prefix	D											
description	HH											

number	13	14	15	16	17	18	19	20	21	22	23
unit/prefix											
description											

Write, in the box alongside, the one missing letter from each of these jumbled words. When these letters are read downwards they spell out three more words. There are clues for these words as well as for the jumbled words.

#	Word	Clue
1	ACAER	An optical instrument used for fixing the image of an object on a light-sensitive film.
2	ATEMGR	Ions do this in solution and cause an electric current.
3	MVAUU	What there is at the top of a Torricellian barometer.
4	EPKEE	A piece of soft iron placed across the ends of a bar magnet to help reduce self-demagnetisation.
5	KCBL	A rectangular glass *this* can be used to show the refraction of light.
6	XEMLAL	He devised a corkscrew rule to show the direction of the magnetic field around a conductor carrying a current.
7	MAGRH	His law of diffusion states that at constant temperature gases diffuse at rates which are inversely proportional to the square roots of their densities.
8	LATREEI	This density is a ratio.
9	REGK	Archimedes was this nationality.
10	TADNICE	Displacement is the vector equivalent of this scalar quantity.
11	BRMA	An area of total shadow.
12	CTKEII	This type of energy equals $\frac{1}{2}mv^2$
13	ACMUIM	A metal used in conjunction with nickel in rechargeable batteries.
14	PUSTP	This type of transformer has more coils on the secondary than the primary. (4,2)
15	LHEAD	If the potential difference across a conductor is reduced from 12 V to 6 V then the current will be this.
16	TOFNRAC	The expansivity of a substance is the _____ of its original length by which it expands per degree rise in temperature.
17	ELNG	The critical *this* for glass is 42°.
18	TEDDO	On ray diagrams lines are drawn *this* to indicate where the rays appear to come from.
19	THCOAD	Positive ions will be attracted to this electrode during electrolysis.
20	SBEN	A bimetallic strip does this when heated.
21	IDEDDI	Pressure is equal to force _____ by area.
22	LUHME	Alpha particles are the nuclei of this element.
23	REWE	He suggested charged particles to explain his theory of electromagnetism.
24	MANOL	A line drawn at 90° to a reflecting surface, from which angles are measured.
25	TICVOL	This pile was capable of causing a current to flow through a conductor.
26	ENUBRI	In a power station this is turned by steam and drives the generators.
27	RESSE	If bulbs are connected in this way, when one goes out they will all go out.
28	NZOE	This layer of the Earth's atmosphere absorbs ultraviolet radiation.
29	AIUURM	Element number 92 in the periodic table.
30	CEEXS	When an object is lowered into a displacement can the _____ water will give the volume of the object.

Extra Clues for Vertical Words

1　These are radio waves of short wavelength and are used in cooking. (10)
2　If a ray of light falls on a glass block so that the angle of incidence is 0° then it will be *this* on entering the block. (10)
3　Sound is produced by *this* of stretched strings. (10)

DOUBLE puzzle

Solve the clues and enter the answers in the Answer Grid. Two vertical words will appear in the first column. There are Extra Clues for these. Transfer the numbered letters to the Reference Check on page 8 and use this to fill in the Message Grid. This Grid will give information about the capacitance of a conductor.

CLUES

1. This is the distance moved in a specified direction. (12)
2. For water this is anomalous between 4°C and 0°C. (9)
3. This chamber in a jet engine is where the fuel is burnt in compressed air. (10)
4. The this or its opposite, the "heaviness", of an object is referred to as its density. (9)
5. Two waves can do this to each other in a constructive or destructive way. (9)
6. This position is located when the image of a pin is found using a search pin. (2,8)
7. This moment will equal the clockwise moment around a point when an object is in equilibrium. (13)
8. In the S.I. system kilo means this. (8)
9. For water this is anomalous between 4°C and 0°C (9)
10. If a tube is this at both ends the first position of resonance will be at a half wavelength. (4)
11. You can do this to a charged rod by drawing it through the ionised air above a flame. (10)
12. Visible to the naked eye. (11)
13. The _____ centre is the middle of the lens. (7)
14. This can be achieved by placing a magnet in a coil of wire carrying an alternating current and slowly withdrawing the magnet. (15)
15. If a volatile liquid does this it causes cooling of the surroundings. (10)
16. The power of a lens is the _____ of its focal length in metres. (10)
17. A light metal with a density of 2700 kg/m³. (9)
18. This control on an oscilloscope causes the electron beam to move horizontally across the screen. (4-4)
19. A centrifugal force will act in an _____ direction. (7)
20. This index is the ratio of the velocity of light in a vacuum to its velocity in the medium it passes through. (10)

PHYSICAL PROCESSES

Extra Clues

First vertical word
The angle between the geographic and magnetic north. (11)

Second vertical word
This is made of graphite and slows down the neutrons in the core of a nuclear reactor. (9)

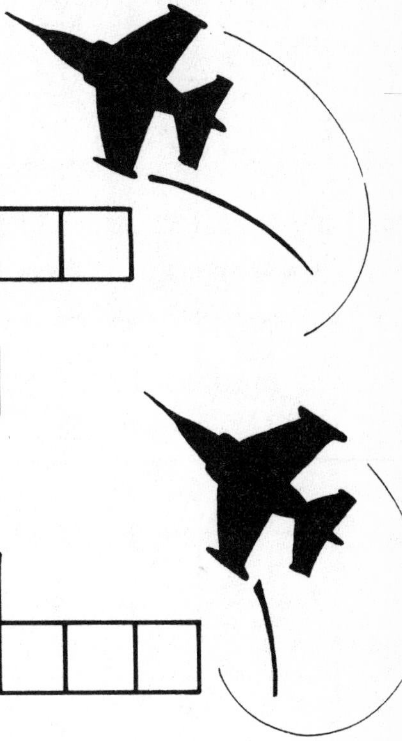

ANSWER GRID

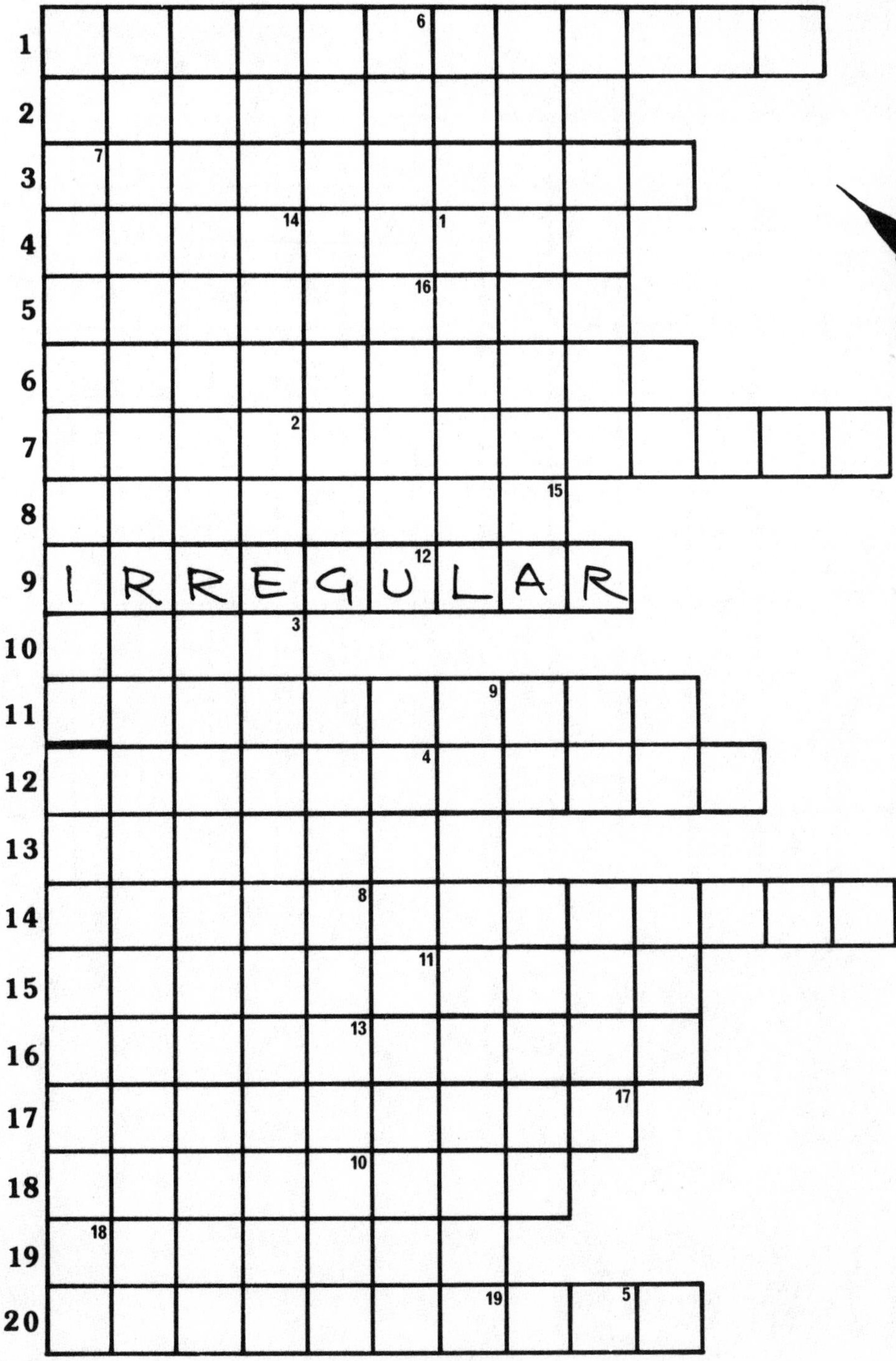

Row 9: I R R E G U L A R

see over

81

Reference Check

1	2	3	4	5
6	7	8	9	10
11	12 U	13	14	15
16	17	18	19	

MESSAGE GRID

19	14	1	●	12 U	3	2	19	●	18	16	●	7	6	13
6	7	2	19	6	3	7	1	●		7	6	9	9	1	15
●	19	14	1	●	16	6	11	6	15	●	2	4	●	15
1	16	2	3	1	15	●	6	4	●	19	14	1	●	7
6	13	6	7	2	19	6	3	7	1	●	18	16	●	6
●	7	18	3	15	12 U	7	19	18	11	●	4	12 U	7	14
●	19	14	6	19	●	6	●	7	14	6	11	8	1	●
18	16	●	18	3	1	●	7	18	12 U	9	18	17	10	●
7	14	6	3	8	1	4	●	2	19	4	●	13	18	19
1	3	19	2	6	9	●	10	Y	●	18	3	1	●	5
18	9	19 ●	●											

Words may start on one line and end on the next. The dots show where words end. Note that the letter Y has been entered into the Grid. Y has no number.

An ABC Crossword

This puzzle consists of twenty-six clues. Each answer begins with a different letter of the alphabet. Solve the clues and arrange the answers in their correct positions in the grid.

CLUES

A For the electrolysis of water to take place a few drops of this are added. (4)

B This French scientist tested fluorescent materials with photographic paper to see if they gave out radiation. (9)

C Heat will always flow from a hot body to a _____ body. (6)

D During electrolysis what is liberated at the anode will be *this* on the cathode. (9)

E The body's camera. (3)

F A vibration consists of a movement to and _____. (3)

G This metal is used in the form of a leaf to hold a charge in an electroscope. (4)

H Temperature is a measure of a body's *this*. (7)

I This when pure and melting establishes the lower fixed point of a thermometer. (3)

J This type of engine burns its fuel in a blast of compressed air so that gases are expelled at very high velocity. (3)

K The unit of temperature on the thermodynamic scale. (6)

L Lenz's *this* said that the direction of the induced current is such as to oppose the change producing it. (3)

M The amount of matter a body contains. (4)

N A gas used in fluorescent tubes which gives an orange-red colour. (4)

O This type of material will not allow the transmission of light. (6)

P Balls of this material are used in electrostatic experiments. (4)

Q This sulphate glows in the presence of ultraviolet light. (7)

R If a charged *this* touches a pith ball the ball becomes charged and is repelled. (3)

S This enables rapidly moving objects to be viewed. (11)

T If you increase the number of these on the secondary coil of a transformer you will increase the E.M.F. (5)

U The direction of the force exerted by water on an object suspended in it. (2)

V The speed of light is 3×10^8 m/s in *this*. (5)

W A parabolic reflector is used in a car headlamp so that the parallel beam produced is *this*. (4)

X In an oscilloscope this is mounted vertically, and so will cause the electron beam to move in a horizontal direction. (1-5)

Y In an electric bell the two soft iron cores are joined by a soft iron *this*. (4)

Z The kinetic energy of a pendulum will be *this* when its amplitude is at a maximum. (4)

Answer each of Clues 1-24 and, starting at the
appropriate clue number, put the answer into the wheel,
radially. The first letter is put in the outer ring and,
since all the answers have eight letters, the last letter of
each answer will be in the inner ring. When you have
completed the wheel, you will find the answers to the
Outer Circle Clues around the outer circle. The inner
circle letters can then be used, as explained, to give the
answers to the Inner Circle Clues.

CLUES

1   At *this* zero molecules possess no kinetic energy.
2   In the oil drop experiment the thickness of the film can be regarded as the *this*
    of the oil molecule.
3   When a ray of light passes through a triangular prism it will be _____ from its
    original path.
4   An object placed at the principal focus of a converging lens will have the image
    in focus here.
5   It is possible to _____ radio waves over long distances because they can be
    reflected by the ionosphere.
6   A choke in a fluorescent tube is an example of an _____.
7   When calculating the linear expansivity of a metal this length of the metal is
    required.
8   These charges are attracted to positive charges.
9   For Boyle's Law to apply, the fixed mass of gas must be at *this* temperature.
10 The _____ _____ square voltage is equal to the peak value of the voltage
    divided by the square root of two. (4,4)
11 Real images will always be this.
12 An electric light bulb will _____ electrical energy into heat and
    light energy.
13 This ray falls on to the reflecting surface.
14 Frequency is the number of *these* oscillations which occur in one second.
15 *This* chloride in the form of a jelly is used in a dry cell.
16 In sound waves the amplitude of the wave will give an indication of this.
17 A measuring *this* is used to find liquid volumes.
18 These charges attract.
19 This gas in the bulb of a filament lamp at low pressure helps prevent evaporation
    of the metal.
20 The Y-plates of an oscilloscope will move the beam in this plane.
21 An _____ prism is used in optical instruments when it is important that the
    image is the correct way up.
22 A variable resistor.
23 On a graph of voltage against current for a conductor, this will give the value of
    the conductor's resistance.
24 This type of field will not deflect gamma radiation.

OUTER CIRCLE CLUES
1-8   Colour mixing by this method is used in pigments.
9-16 If this angle is exceeded when light is travelling from glass to air then total
      internal reflection occurs.
17-24 Parallel rays of light will do this when they pass through a convex lens.

INNER CIRCLE CLUES

To answer these clues you must add 3 As, 2 Is, 3 Os and 1 U to the letters already in the inner circle. Don't use the ones in the shaded sections.

1 Mercury is 13.6 times more *this* than water. (5)
2 This is defined as the distance travelled by light in a vacuum in 1/300 000 000 of a second. (5)
3 These electromagnetic waves come from high-frequency oscillatory electric circuits. (5)
4 Refractive index is an example of a *this*. (5)
5 The _____ rate indicates the activity of a radioactive source. (5)
6 _____ diagrams locate images in optics. (3)

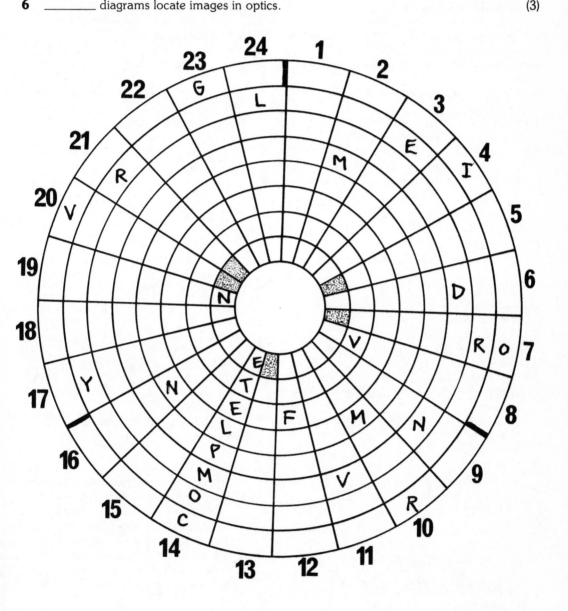

Answer the clues and fill in the horizontal lines of the appropriate grid. A word, which is also clued, will be formed diagonally, from top left, across the block. One or two letters have been entered in each block, to help you.

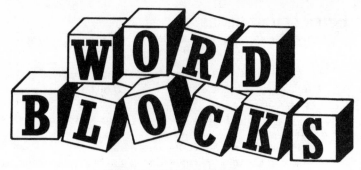

(A) DIAGONAL CLUE
This quantity has magnitude only.
1 This type of balance can be calibrated to measure the force of gravity on a mass.
2 A virtual image cannot be produced on one.
3 These rely on friction to bring moving objects to rest.
4 A normal is always drawn at right _____ to the incident surface.
5 In a virtual image the rays of light only _____ to come from the image.
6 If an object is placed between a convex lens and its focal length the image will be _____ than the object.

(B) DIAGONAL CLUE
This type of mirror can be convex, concave or parabolic.
1 The focal length of a lens is the distance from the principal focus to the *this*.
2 In the eye there is vitreous and aqueous.
3 _____ of parallax should be avoided when measuring with a scale.
4 This type of lens is also called converging.
5 An object capable of attracting iron, steel, cobalt and nickel.
6 In a transformer, efficiency is improved by ensuring that all the primary flux is *this* with the secondary.

(C) DIAGONAL CLUE
The amount of space an object takes up.
1 When water is heated, at 100°C the water will change from a liquid to *this* if the atmospheric pressure is normal.
2 A beam can be made to do this if it is pivoted at one end and a force is applied to the other.
3 If a mercury barometer is *this* the vertical height of the mercury in the tube stays the same.
4 In this state the molecules of a material take the shape of the container, but need not fill it.
5 A device for producing electric current by electromagnetic induction.
6 If you _____ the electrons of an object you leave it with a positive charge.

(D) DIAGONAL CLUE
A non-metallic conductor of electricity.
1 The presence of *this* can be detected by a gold leaf electroscope.
2 One of these is a pressure of 1 N/m^2.
3 Ferromagnetic materials have this type of attraction to a magnet.
4 If you double the length of a wire you will _____ the resistance.
5 Newton's third law of *this* simply states that to every action there is an equal and opposite reaction.
6 One of these will give a mass of 1 kilogram an acceleration of 1 m/s^2.

(E) DIAGONAL CLUE
If you do this to the thickness of a wire you will increase its resistance.
1 This is propelled forwards in space by exhaust gases being ejected at high velocity in the opposite direction.
2 The temperature of an object is a number which expresses its *this* of hotness on a particular scale.
3 Latent heat is this.
4 This can be found at the top of a Torricellian barometer tube.
5 The magnetic _____ of a current was discovered by Oersted.
6 A _____, released at the bottom of a deep liquid-filled tank, will increase in volume as it rises to the surface.

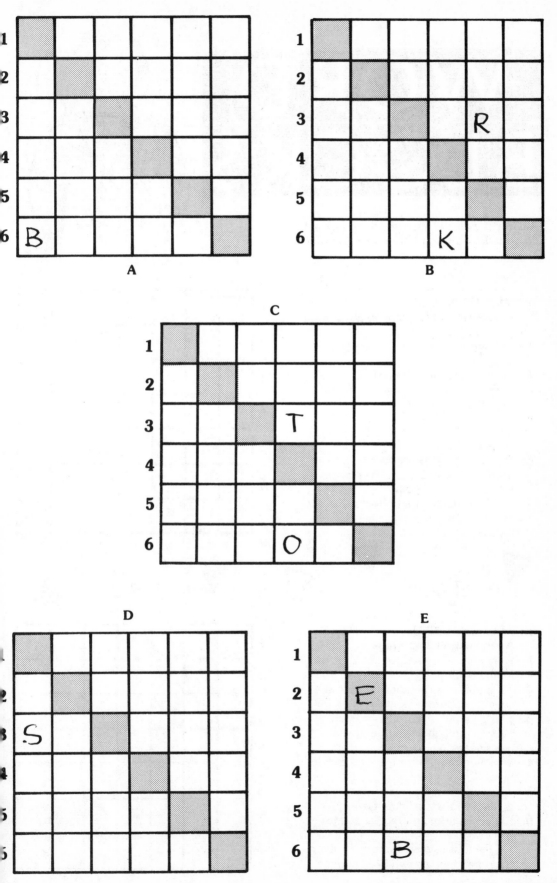

WORD BLOCKS

Answer the clues. A word will be formed diagonally, from top left, across the block.

(A) DIAGONAL CLUE

In a camera this opens to allow light through the aperture.

1 *This* tension is reduced by adding detergent.
2 An ion is this type of particle.
3 These conduct the current from the slip-rings of a dynamo.
4 A series of cells joined together.
5 It is connected in series and measures current in a circuit.
6 A virtual image is produced when an object is placed _____ a convex lens and its focal point.
7 *This* magnitude of an object is the angle it subtends at the eye.

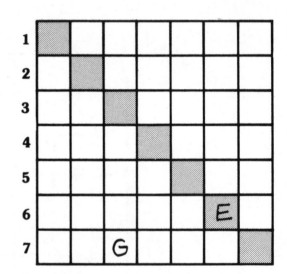

(B) DIAGONAL CLUE

A direction-finding magnet.

1 A thermostat is used to _____ the temperature.
2 This, unlike evaporation, occurs at a set temperature for a given pressure.
3 *This* pressure is caused by a liquid passing through a semi-permeable membrane.
4 This type of surface makes an inclined plane.
5 *This* velocity is the total distance divided by the total time taken.
6 Reflection from an irregular surface is *this*.
7 On the Celsius scale there are 100 of these between the two fixed points.

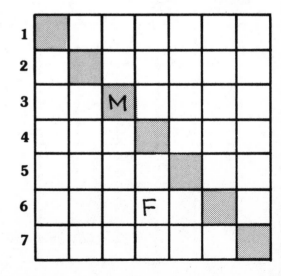

88

(C) DIAGONAL CLUE

The splitting of a uranium atom.

1 A statement of scientific facts using symbols.
2 Iron _____ are used to show magnetic field patterns.
3 This part of the electromagnetic spectrum contains the seven colours of light.
4 A potassium permanganate *this* dropped into water can demonstrate convection currents.
5 This relies on the frictional forces between surfaces to stop a moving vehicle.
6 A volatile liquid used in a cloud chamber to produce a supersaturated vapour.
7 *This* in a vertical string is caused by the force of gravity on the load on the end of the string.

(D) DIAGONAL CLUE

A penumbra is this type of shadow.

1 The input coil of a transformer.
2 The potential energy is *this* when a pendulum is at its greatest amplitude.
3 Virtual images are always *this*.
4 Ohm stated that at constant temperature this is proportional to the current through the conductor.
5 *These* powders, used in the home, often contain a substance which fluoresces under ultraviolet light.
6 If the moments about a point are *this* then turning will occur.
7 This type of image cannot be produced on a screen.

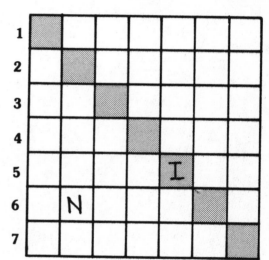

WORD BLOCKS

Answer the clues. A word will be formed diagonally, from top left, across the block.

(A) DIAGONAL CLUE
A composition of two or more metals.

1 The positive electrode.
2 This coloured surface radiates the most heat.
3 In a Geiger Müller tube, when ionisation occurs, a *this* of current is produced which can be counted by a scaler.
4 Steel rods containing *this* are used as control rods in a nuclear reaction.
5 An electromagnetic device used in a circuit using only a small current to switch on a circuit carrying a large current.

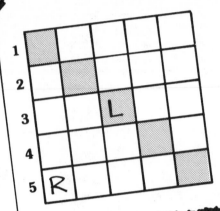

(B) DIAGONAL CLUE
The armature is the *these* of a dynamo.

1 This type of reaction can occur when a neutron splits a uranium atom.
2 A lens is used in a camera to ensure that the image is in *this* on the film.
3 What we call the electricity supply to households.
4 To convert a galvanometer into an ammeter a shunt having a _____ resistance is connected in parallel with the meter.
5 In ray diagrams, where rays from the object do this, the image will be formed.

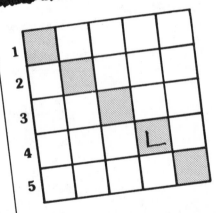

(C) DIAGONAL CLUE
A photographic *this* is affected by radioactive materials.

1 Rate of working.
2 Wood will do this in water because it is less dense than water.
3 This material has a refractive index of about 1.5.
4 These in solution will conduct electricity.
5 A push or pull.

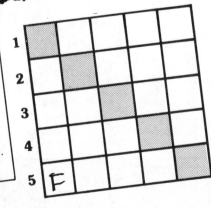

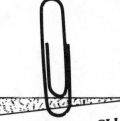

(D) DIAGONAL CLUE
To convert a galvanometer to a _____ voltmeter a multiplier with a _____ resistance is connected in series with the meter.

1 These electromagnetic waves consist of seven colours.
2 For alpha particles *this* is only a few centimetres in air.
3 A graph to show radioactive decay will be an exponential *this*.
4 A Bourdon _____ is used to measure the pressure of fluids.
5 Also called the gradient of a graph.

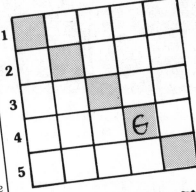

(E) DIAGONAL CLUE
Found by dividing distance by time.

1 The volume of this type of object can be found by displacement.
2 The displacement water from a Eureka can flows through this.
3 Used to drive the turbine in a coal-fired power station.
4 This type of jack is often used for lifting cars, but is of very low efficiency.
5 A _____ chamber may be used to detect the presence of charged particles.

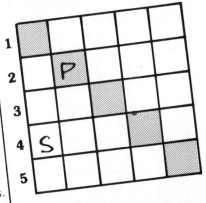

(F) DIAGONAL CLUE
This type of internal reflection is used in a prism periscope.

1 In the right-hand grip rule this points in the direction of the current.
2 If you do this to a charged electroscope you will earth it.
3 This liquid has its maximum density at 4°C.
4 Copper is an example.
5 In a manometer the liquid in the two arms should be *this* at the start of the experiment.

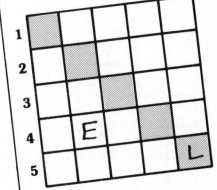

WORD BLOCKS

Answer the clues. A word will be formed diagonally, from top left, across the block.

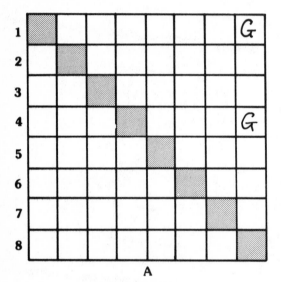

A

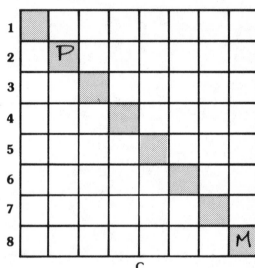

C

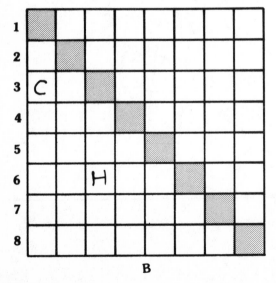

B

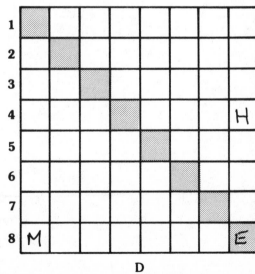

D

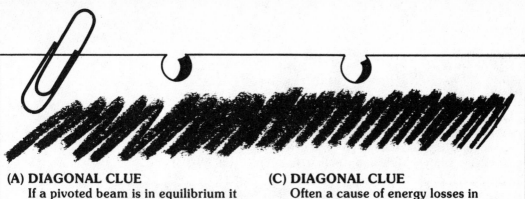

(A) DIAGONAL CLUE
If a pivoted beam is in equilibrium it will be this.

1 This of the skin is a result of ultraviolet radiation.
2 When a rocket moves, the forward momentum of the rocket is equal and opposite to the _____ momentum of the exhaust gases.
3 *This* of a light bulb is made of a metal with a high melting point.
4 A _____ body displaces its own weight of the fluid which it is in.
5 Rays of light which produce an image at the focal point can be considered to have come from *this* distance.
6 This type of decomposition occurs as a result of electrolysis.
7 This type of balloon floats in air because of the upthrust of the air.
8 The force of gravity acts in this direction.

(B) DIAGONAL CLUE
The visible one contains seven colours.

1 *This* pressure is 760 mm of mercury.
2 Interference patterns from a diffraction grating depend on the _____ of the slits.
   Pressure in a gas will increase if the particles' collisions with the wall of the container become more _____.
4 When an object is resting on the ground this is the force which is equal and opposite to the weight.
5 An electrolytic *this* conducts electricity.
6 This material does not retain its magnetism. (4,4)
7 At the extremes of its swing its potential energy is a maximum and its kinetic energy is zero.
8 The metal used for the electrodes in a Hoffmann voltameter.

(C) DIAGONAL CLUE
Often a cause of energy losses in machines.

1 This type of rectification is brought about by a bridge rectifier. (4,4)
2 The efficiency of a motor can be increased by winding the coils on a soft iron *this* because it gives extra magnetic flux to the coil.
3 If an object is placed at the radius of curvature of a concave mirror the object and image will _____.
4 This material is used for the shield in a nuclear reactor.
5 This stroke in the four-stroke cycle of a petrol engine follows compression.
6 *These* forces occur between molecules of the same substance.
7 Thermionic _____ is the process by which electrons leave a hot filament.
8 A charged particle which, when it drifts through a conductor, causes a current.

(D) DIAGONAL CLUE
When a liquid is heated every _____ will gain kinetic energy.

1 Lodestone is an example of such a mineral ore.
2 Negative ions will be attracted to this terminal during electrolysis.
3 Amount of pressure equal to one thousandth of a bar.
4 This of a magnetic field induced into a soft iron rod by an electric current, can be increased by increasing the number of turns on the coil.
5 Speed in a given direction.
6 At *this* zero the molecules of a substance will have no kinetic energy.
7 To find the force on an object, _____ the pressure by the area.
8 Radioactive tracers can have uses in industry and also this branch of science.

2's + 3's

Complete the crossword in the normal way. However, your answers must be written with two or three letters in each square. Any single letters have been given to you to start you off. One answer and some double and treble letters have been filled in.

CLUES ACROSS

1 Railway lines can suffer *this* if no allowance is made for expansion. (10)

4 The inner surfaces of a vacuum flask are coated with this metal to reduce heat loss or gain through radiation. (6)

5 *This* of air around a room can be caused by convection currents. (11)

7 The oil-film experiment will allow you to find the thickness of one. (8)

9 Rubbing glass with this will give a positive charge. (4)

10 A machine which produces an electric current by electromagnetic induction. (9)

11 To every *this* there is an equal and opposite reaction. (6)

12 This material when mixed gives different colours by subtractive colour mixing. (5)

13 A _____ of water can provide a pressure. (4)

14 Power is defined as the *this* of energy transfer. (4)

15 An object has potential energy because of its *this*. (8)

18 If sine i is plotted against sine r on a _____ you will get a straight line. (5)

19 An anode or a cathode. (9)

21 Charles' Law states that, for a fixed mass of gas at constant pressure, the volume and thermodynamic temperature are *this* to each other. (12)

22 This type of current is needed to operate a transformer. (11)

26 The capacity to perform work. (6)

27 A solar _____ is caused by the moon passing between the Earth and the Sun. (7)

29 The law of conservation of momentum states that the momentum before and _____ the collision are equal. (5)

30 This converts sound energy into electrical energy. (10)

31 An _____ is made up of protons, neutrons and electrons. (4)

34 Force per unit area. (8)

37 Used to find the position of an image. (3)

38 The vacuum at the top of a mercury barometer was named after this Italian. (10)

39 This occurs when light passes from one optical medium to another. (10)

40 Petrol is mixed with *this* so that it can be burnt in a car engine. (3)

CLUES DOWN

1 The splitting of white light into a spectrum. (10)

2 An object is elastic if it returns to its _____ shape and size. (8)

3 A complete to and fro movement is called an _____. (11)

4 This touch method gives a steel needle different poles at each end. (6)

6 *This* will happen between a positive and negative charge. (10)

7 This satellite's gravitational pull on the Earth's oceans causes the tides. (4)

8 Ohm's Law states that *this* is proportional to voltage at constant temperature. (7)

10 The _____ position of an object will affect the force of gravity acting on it. (12)

13 Latent _____ is involved when a change of state occurs. (4)

15 This type of energy equals *mgh*. (9)

16 This is achieved in a nuclear reactor by using a thick layer of concrete. (9)

17 Negative charges are attracted to this. (5)

20 Heat is _____ from a body at one temperature to a body at a lower temperature. (11)

21 An object impelled by a force in both a horizontal and vertical direction. (10)

23 A measurement of a body's "hotness" on a particular scale. (11)

24 This number indicates how many protons are present in the nucleus of an atom. (6)

25 The earpiece of this instrument uses a changing magnetic field to cause a diaphragm to vibrate. (9)

28 Germanium is an example of one. (13)

32 This square law explains the effect on the count rate of moving the source away from a Geiger-Müller counter. (7)

33 These are the S.I. units of time. (7)

34 A _____ plane is used to transfer a small sample charge from a conductor to an electroscope for testing. (5)

35 This type of current comes from a cell. (6)

36 Two positive charges will _____ each other. (5)

DOUBLES and TREBLES

Complete the 28 words below. If a letter occurs in a word
more than once it has been given to you. All the rest are
missing. The missing letters are given in the box on page 97.

1 C _ _ C _
When measuring the time taken for an object to fall a
short distance you need a very accurate one.

2 _ O _ O _
This consists of a coil of wire carrying a current which
is placed in a magnetic field and made to rotate.

3 P _ P _ _
Several sheets of *this* can be used to absorb alpha
radiation.

4 V _ _ V _
A diode acts as one.

5 _ _ _ _ E _ E
One flows when the rate of charge past a point is
6×10^{18} electrons.

6 _ _ _ EE _ E
Convection currents can cause an on- or off-shore
this.

7 _ _ PP _ _
A good electrical conductor with a density of 8900
kg/m³.

8 _ _ _ MM _ _ _
A claw *this* can act as a lever.

9 _ _ _ TT _ _ _
It can exist in any of three states.

10 M _ _ _ _ _ M
Refraction occurs when light passes from one
optical *this* to another.

11 _ UT _ UT
For a perfect transformer the energy input will be
equal to *this* energy.

12 _ T _ T _ _
This type of electricity can be found on objects
after they have been rubbed.

13 _ A _ A _ _ _
A spring *this* can be used to measure the force of
gravity on a mass.

14 CI _ C _ I _
In order for a current to flow through an electric
bulb from a cell there must be a complete one.

15 _ _ R _ _ R _
A dense metal, liquid at room temperature, which
is used in barometers.

16 _ E _ _ I _ IE _
A current can be *this* by using diodes.

17 R _ _ _ _ _ _ R
In a nuclear *this*, the heat produced may be used
to make electricity.

18 _ _ I _ - _ I _ _
This takes the current from an A.C. generator.

19 D _ _ _ _ _ _ D _
These can be made to fluoresce when ultraviolet
radiation shines on them.

20 _ A _ _ - _ A _ _
This type of rectification can be carried out by a
single diode.

21 _ A _ A _ _ _ A
Reflectors in the shape of *this* are used for headlamp

22 _ A _ A L L _ L
Rays of this type will converge to the principal
focus after passing through a convex lens.

23 _ _ _ R _ -E _ EC _ R _ C
The type of power station which uses stored
water.

24 _ _ _ _ _ ET _ TE
A magnetic form of iron ore also called lodestone.

25 HE _ _ S _ HE _ ES
Otto von Guericke used two to demonstrate the
pressure of the atmosphere.

26 PERPE _ _ _ _ _ _ _ _ R
The displacement of a transverse wave is *this* to
the direction of the movement.

27 PE _ _ _ _ _ PE
A prism *this* uses total internal reflection in two
45° prisms.

28 _ E _ _ _ NEN _
Steel is used for magnets which are *this*.

MISSING LETTERS

SAIC
COER
RUT
MIPR
PRMAT
EACTO
HAER
MECUY
SLPRNG
AER
LOK
BLNCE
NDICULA
MAER
PRBOL
IAMONS
AMPR
HYDOLTI
MAGNI
PRE
RISCO
BRZ
MTR
ALE
RCTFD
EDIU
HLFWVE
OP

THE NUMBERS GAME

The statements and the numbers have been mixed up. Can you sort them out? Put the correct number in the space provided.

1 The distance across our galaxy. 3
2 The amount of oxygen by mass that can be found in the water on Earth. .... 10^{-7} m
3 The distance across the universe. .... 10^{23} km
4 Arachnids have this many pairs of legs. 4
5 The distance of the Earth from the sun. .... 10^{18} km
6 The height that a giant sequoia can reach. .... 100 metres
7 The diameter of the planet Earth. .... 4 light years
8 The diameter of a virus. 89%
9 The distance of the nearest star from the planet Earth. .... 10^{10} km
10 The distance of Mercury from the sun. .... 13,000 km
11 The number of planets in our solar system. 150,000,000
12 The time the Earth takes to complete one orbit around the sun. 9
13 The time that Pluto takes to complete one orbit around the sun. .... 1 year
14 Insects have this many pairs of legs. .... 50,000,000 km
15 The number of stars in our galaxy. .... 27.3 days
16 The time taken by the moon to orbit the Earth. .... 100 billion
17 The diameter of our solar system. .... 6,000°C
18 The temperature on the surface of the sun. .... 250 years
19 The approximate number of cells in your body. 100,000,000
20 The distance light travels every second. .... 300,000 km
21 The average time taken for a blood cell to circulate around the body. 23%
22 The distance of Pluto from the Sun. 99%
23 The approximate number of heart-beats a minute. .... 45 secs
24 The sun accounts for this amount of the solar system's mass. 70
25 Coal, oil and natural gas yield about this amount of the fuel required by our homes and industry. 700
26 The temperature at the centre of the sun. .... 500,000,000 km
27 The approximate number of red blood cells to every white blood cell. 46
28 The number of elements known today. .... 14,000,000°C
29 The amount of oxygen by mass that can be found in the Earth's atmosphere. 80%
30 The diploid number of chromosomes in a human cell. 105

THE NUMBERS GAME

The statements and the
numbers have been mixed
up. Can you sort them
out? Put the correct
number in the space
provided.

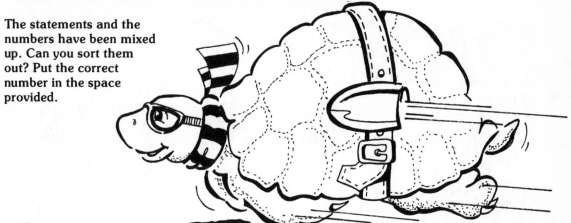

1	The speed of the fastest bird on earth (spine-tailed swift).	.... 13 m/s
2	The speed of a tortoise.	.... 1.6×10^{-19}
3	The amount of oxygen in the air by volume.	.... 10N
4	The amount of nitrogen in the air by volume.	.... 9.8 m/s^2
5	The speed of the fastest land vehicle.	 3,600,00
6	The speed of the fastest fish.	.... 100N/m^2
7	The amount of noble gases in the air by volume.	.... 47m/s
8	The speed of air molecules at room temperature.	 240
9	The speed of a rocket escaping from the Earth's gravitational field.	.... 760 mm
10	The speed of light.	.... 0.08
11	One mole of copper is deposited by this number of coulombs.	.... 250mm
12	The speed of the fastest human sprinter.	.... 21%
13	The charge of one electron measured in coulombs.	 1013
14	The weight of an object with a mass of 1kg.	.... 30A
15	The acceleration due to gravity.	.... 78%
16	The number of joules in one kilowatt hour.	.... 3A
17	The pressure one millibar is equal to.	.... 330m/s
18	The number of volts of electricity supplied by the mains.	.... 0.75
19	The height reached by a column of mercury which is commonly quoted as being equal to the atmospheric pressure.	.... 300,000,000 m/s
20	The height of a column of mercury recorded at the top of Everest.	 193,000
21	The number of millibars that the standard atmospheric pressure is equal to.	.... 13A
22	The ring main is protected by this size of fuse.	.... 10^{-10}m
23	Appliances like table lamps and television sets should have this size of fuse.	.... 0.9%
24	Kettles, irons and electric fires should have this size of fuse.	.... 500 m/s
25	The number of kilowatts that are equal to 1 horse power.	.... 11,000 m/s
26	The diameter of the smallest atom.	.... 27 m/s
27	The speed of the fastest land animal.	.... 30 m/s
28	The wavelength of the medium wave band of radio waves.	.... 20,000 Hz
29	The lowest frequency of sound that a human ear can hear.	.... 3×10^{-2}m
30	The highest frequency of sound that a human ear can hear.	.... 20 Hz

Match the scientists to the dated discoveries. Enter your answers in the grid, writing the proper scientist letter under each discovery number.

FAMOUS SCIENTISTS

A   Bombarded uranium with neutrons — it was the first time an atom was "split".
B   Discovered radioactivity.
C   Described the conditions needed for hydrogen and nitrogen to react to produce ammonia commercially.
D   Predicted the properties of elements and produced the modern version of the periodic table.
E   Built the first spectrometer.
F   Scientist who destroyed the old belief in four basic elements.
G   Discovered oxygen.
H   Described the nucleus of an atom.
I   Built the first atomic reactor.
J   Put forward the Law of Conservation of Mass.
K   Found that every eighth element in the periodic table was similar; called them octaves.
L   Discovered the radioactive elements radium and polonium.
M   Suggested elements could be grouped in threes — called triads.
N   Discovered cathode rays.
O   Discovered neon, krypton and xenon.
P   Discovered neutrons.
Q   Described movement of pollen grains in water.
R   First described and named the atom.

1	1661	Robert Boyle
2	1774	Antoine Lavoisier
3	1774	Joseph Priestley
4	1807	John Dalton
5	1827	Robert Brown
6	1829	Johann Döbereiner
7	1864	John Newlands
8	1869	Dmitri Mendeleev
9	1896	Henri Becquerel
10	1897	Joseph John Thomson
11	1898	Pierre and Marie Curie
12	1898	Sir William Ramsay
13	1908	Fritz Haber
14	1911	Ernest Rutherford
15	1919	Francis Aston
16	1932	James Chadwick
17	1938	Otto Hahn and Fritz Strassman
18	1942	Enrico Fermi

Famous Scientists

Below are the surnames of famous scientists and their discoveries. Unfortunately they are mixed up. Can you sort them out? Enter your answers in the grid provided.

1	BOYLE	A	Swedish scientist who introduced the basis for modern taxonomy in 1753.
2	HOOKE	B	The number of atoms in a mole is this constant number of 6×10^{23}.
3	FARADAY	C	Scientist who found the atomic particle called a proton.
4	MILLIKAN	D	The first scientist to transmit radio signals over long distances.
5	OHM	E	Scientist who discovered cathode rays.
6	GILBERT	F	His law states that the extension of a spring is proportional to the stretching force.
7	AVOGADRO	G	The method for manufacturing ammonia was developed by this scientist.
8	MENDELEEV	H	His constant is equal to 96,500 coulombs.
9	MARCONI	I	He discovered the blood circulation.
10	DARWIN	J	Introduced the word element.
11	HABER	K	He discovered the atomic particle called a neutron.
12	THOMPSON	L	The unit of resistance is named after this scientist.
13	RUTHERFORD	M	The scientist who put forward the theory of natural selection.
14	CHADWICK	N	His process is used to extract sulphur from underground deposits by melting it.
15	ASTON	O	He found the charge on an electron was 1.6×10^{-19} coulombs.
16	FERMI	P	He first used the terms positive and negative.
17	FRASCH	Q	This scientist thought the Earth behaved as if a giant magnet was buried at its centre.
18	FRANKLIN	R	An Austrian physicist who noticed that the pitch of a note changes as the sound approaches then passes you.
19	GUERICKE	S	The first small atomic reactor was built by this Italian.
20	DOPPLER	T	He arranged the elements in order of atomic mass.
21	BECQUEREL	U	Scientist who made a model of metals out of soap bubbles.
22	BRAGG	V	Scientist who built the first mass spectrometer.
23	OERSTED	W	Monk called father of genetics.
24	MENDEL	X	The first person to discover that a bell could not be heard ringing in a vacuum.
25	HARVEY	Y	A Danish professor who discovered that a current in a wire has a magnetic effect.
26	LINNAEUS	Z	The scientist who first discovered radioactivity.

A	B	C	D	E	F	G	H	I	J	K	L	M

N	O	P	Q	R	S	T	U	V	W	X	Y	Z

ANSWERS

Solve and Fit

An A.B.C. of Biology

The Wheel

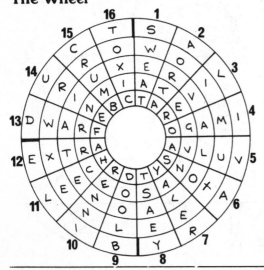

OUTER CIRCLE WORDS
These are SALIVARY and BILE DUCT and they help to digest the inner words, which, when unscrambled, read CARBOHYDRATE and FATS.

Missing Letters

PUZZLE 4

1
P	HAPLOID
R	CARDIAC
O	BOMB
S	AEROSOLS
T	ARTERIOLES
A	A.T.P.
T	CATALYST
E	FLAGELLA

2
C	ARACHNID
O	BROAD
W	GROWTH
P	CROP
E	DUODENUM
R	BARBS
S	ANUS

3
S	CYST
E	CHYME
M	AMINO
I	AURICLES
N	CANINE
A	A.D.H.
L	BULB
V	CERVIX
E	CORTEX
S	EMULSIFY
I	AXIL
C	BICONCAVE
L	CALYX
E	DIGEST

4
T	EGESTION
E	CARIES
S	FISH
T	D.D.T.
I	BIENNIAL
S	FALSE

Missing Letters

PUZZLE 5

O	cone
E	operculum
S	oestrogen
O	abiotic
P	adipose
H	alcohol
A	auxin
G	graafian
U	mucus
S	lysozyme
S	osmosis
T	genotype
O	corm
M	chyme
A	hypha
C	ascorbic
H	hypothalamus

D	adenine
U	albumen
O	dorsal
D	disc
E	epiglottis
N	essential
U	fluoride
M	ferment
I	Benedict's
L	pupil
E	pine
U	guanine
M	germinate

C	bacteria
O	locust
L	leaf
O	kingdom
N	bronchioles
R	drone
E	hammer
C	duct
T	antigens
U	plaque
M	lymph

A Mix-Up A-M

PUZZLE 6

A	B	C	D	E	F	G	H	I	J	K	L	M	N	O
23	29	24	20	11	4	22	5	6	19	7	8	21	9	2

P	Q	R	S	T	U	V	W	X	Y	Z	a	b	c	d
16	15	14	18	25	12	1	3	17	30	28	27	26	10	13

A Mix-Up N-Z

A	B	C	D	E	F	G	H	I	J	K	L	M	N	O
14	27	12	11	10	1	15	8	2	28	3	25	30	4	21

P	Q	R	S	T	U	V	W	X	Y	Z	a	b	c	d
9	5	29	6	16	7	13	24	20	22	17	26	19	18	23

First and Last

AmmoniuM
RelaY
TeaR
HomeostasIs
RetinA
OviParous
PoliO
OmmatiDia
DnA
CiliA
RepaiR
UreA
SaC
ToucH
AdrenaliN
CortI
EyeliD
AmoebA

Reading down the first letters, the words are **ARTHROPOD** and **CRUSTACEA.**

Reading down the last letters, the words are **MYRIAPODA** and **ARACHNIDA.**

Triangles

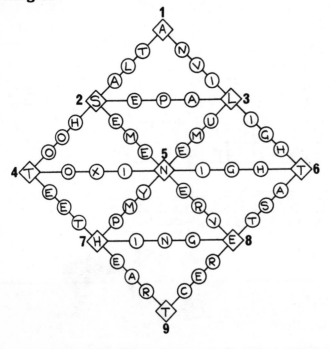

Word Blocks

A
1. KERATIN
2. FILTERS
3. CENTRUM
4. GANGLIA
5. BLADDER
6. EROSION
7. TROPISM

B
1. OVARY
2. TRACE
3. NODES
4. RUMEN
5. OUTER

C
1. FAECES
2. SALIVA
3. CEMENT
4. RETINA
5. VENULE
6. ENERGY

D
1. GREEN
2. DECAY
3. SANDY
4. VIRUS
5. DOWNS

E
1. CROWN
2. BLIND
3. CHALK
4. CROSS
5. BONES

F
1. SEGMENT
2. OPSONIN
3. ASEXUAL
4. TRACHEA
5. PEPTIDE
6. DILATED
7. RICKETS

G
1. PELVIC
2. SHIVER
3. OXYGEN
4. REFLEX
5. RECTUM
6. PHLOEM

A **KINGDOM**
B **ORDER**
C **FAMILY**
D **GENUS**
E **CLASS**
F **SPECIES**
G **PHYLUM**

Word Blocks

A
REFRACT
CILIARY
LACTEAL
SMOKING
COWPERS
STOMATA
NUCLEUS

B
ALVEOLI
INCISOR
CHALAZA
ADRENAL
ENZYMES
INSULIN
DAPHNIA

C
BALANCED
CERVICAL
AEROFOIL
ANTIBODY
CEREBRUM
COMPLETE
AUDITORY
NUCLEOLI

D
PARASITE
DENDRITE
FILTRATE
PHALANGE
BOUYANCY
DIVERGES
PRESSURE
PLACENTA

E
SCLERA
SCALES
NEURAL
UTERUS
ACTIVE
THIRTY

A **RICKETS**
B **ANAEMIA**
C **BERIBERI**
D **PELLAGRA**
E **SCURVY**

Biological Message

Reference Check

1	2	3	4	5	6	7	8	9	10	11	12	13	14	15	16	17	18	19	20	21	22
C	A	B	D	T	O	R	E	U	M	H	Y	I	L	N	P	G	S	V	F	Z	W

CARBOHYDRATE — 1, 2, 7, 3, 6, 11, 12, 4, 7, 2, 5, 8
HUMIDITY — 11, 9, 10, 13, 4, 13, 5, 12
ALIMENTARY — 2, 14, 13, 10, 8, 15, 5, 2, 7, 12
REPRODUCE — 7, 8, 16, 7, 6, 4, 9, 1, 8
LEGUMES — 14, 8, 17, 9, 10, 8, 18
ECDYSIS — 8, 1, 4, 12, 18, 13, 18
SEVENTEEN — 18, 8, 19, 8, 15, 5, 8, 8, 15
DEFECATION — 4, 8, 20, 8, 1, 2, 5, 13, 6, 15
ADVENTITIOUS — 2, 4, 19, 8, 15, 5, 13, 5, 13, 6, 9, 18
RHIZOMES — 7, 11, 13, 21, 6, 10, 8, 18
WOMB — 22, 6, 10, 3
INTESTINES — 13, 15, 5, 8, 18, 5, 13, 15, 8, 18
NECTARY — 15, 8, 1, 5, 2, 7, 12
NITROGENOUS — 15, 13, 5, 7, 6, 17, 8, 15, 6, 9, 18
ANAPHASE — 2, 15, 2, 16, 11, 2, 18, 8
TEETH — 5, 8, 8, 5, 11
URETHRA — 9, 7, 8, 5, 11, 7, 2
ROUGHAGE — 7, 6, 9, 17, 11, 2, 17, 8
ARTHROPOD — 2, 7, 5, 11, 7, 6, 16, 6, 4
LEAF — 14, 8, 2, 20
SELF — 18, 8, 14, 20
EVERGREEN — 8, 19, 8, 7, 17, 7, 8, 8, 15
LYMPH — 14, 12, 10, 16, 11
EPIDERMIS — 8, 16, 13, 4, 8, 7, 10, 13, 18
CLAVICLE — 1, 14, 2, 19, 13, 1, 14, 8
TSETSE — 5, 18, 8, 5, 18, 8
INFLORESCENCE — 13, 15, 20, 14, 6, 7, 8, 18, 1, 8, 15, 18
OESOPHAGUS — 6, 8, 18, 6, 16, 11, 2, 17, 9, 18,
NITRIFYING — 15, 13, 5, 7, 13, 20, 12, 13, 15, 17

Reading down the first letters of the answers
Famous scientist: **Charles Darwin.**
Theory: **natural selection.**

True or False

1 True
2 False ATP contains three molecules of phosphate.
3 True
4 False it is called a biennial.
5 False an earthworm is hermaphrodite male and female; it reproduces sexually.
6 True
7 False plant cells are the only ones with cellulose cell-walls.
8 True
9 False they are called proteins.
10 False fluorine is added to toothpaste.
11 True
12 True
13 True

Bits and Pieces

1 GLUCOSE
2 RENNIN
3 EUSTACHIAN
4 GAMETES
5 OPTIC
6 RIBOSOMES
7 METAMORPHOSIS
8 ENAMEL
9 NODE
10 DENATURES
11 ENDOCRINE
12 LYMPHOCYTE

GREGOR MENDEL

Can be described as a MONK

Who was CALLED THE

FATHER OF GENETICS

Twos and Threes

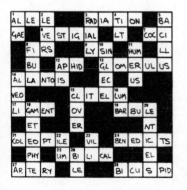

Twos and Threes

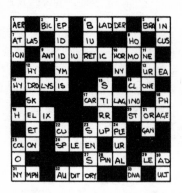

Double Puzzle

Answer grid

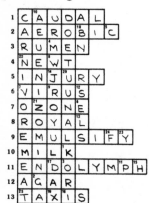

```
1  C A U D A L
2  A E R O B I C
3  R U M E N
4  N E W T
5  I N J U R Y
6  V I R U S
7  O Z O N E
8  R O Y A L
9  E M U L S I F Y
10 M I L K
11 E N D O L Y M P H
12 A G A R
13 T A X I S
```

Extra clues

1 **CARNIVORE**
2 **MEAT**

Reference Check

1	2	3	4	5	6	7	8	9	10	11	12
K	G	O	M	C	E	V	W	R	A	P	S

13	14	15	16	17	18	19	20	21	22	23	24	25
L	J	H	I	D	B	X	U	Z	N	Y	F	T

Message grid

```
JOINTS WHICH ALLOW MOVEMENT
ARE CALLED SYNOVIAL EXAMPL
ES INCLUDE THE HINGE JOINT
OF THE KNEE OR ELBOW AND TH
E BALL AND SOCKET JOINT OF
THE HIP AND SHOULDER SYNOVI
AL FLUID AND CARTILAGE LUBR
ICATE THE MOVEMENT OF THE B
ONES
```

Misspelt

1	WORKER	16	SPHINCTER
2	WILTS	17	RIBS
3	VITAMINS	18	RADIUS
4	VEIN	19	PUBERTY
5	VAGINA	20	PULSE
6	TENDON	21	PULMONARY
7	TRYPSIN	22	POTOMETER
8	TROPHIC	23	PANCREAS
9	TONGUE	24	MYRIAPODS
10	TURGID	25	MYCELIUM
11	STAPES	26	MEASLY
12	STOMACH	27	LOAM
13	SETAE	28	LATERAL
14	SPONGY	29	LENS
15	SACRAL	30	IODINE

The Numbers Game

1	1.5 litres	16	1g/l
2	39 kj/g	17	7000
3	1%	18	0.7 second
4	74%	19	14
5	36.8°	20	22
6	32	21	28 days
7	30 litres	22	20-20 000 HZ
8	2-3000	23	2
9	0.04%	24	1.5 litres
10	43 dioptres	25	90%
11	12	26	20
12	5-6 litres	27	16 dioptres
13	2-3 months	28	7.4
14	4	29	0.5 litres
15	2890kj/mole	30	7

Missing Letter

CHLOROFLUOROCOMPOUNDSAEROSOLS

- CUTICLE
- LICHEN
- HENLÉ
- OMNIVORE
- CORNEA
- OCCLUDED
- FIXING
- FLOW
- PHYLUM
- ORGANISMS
- HEART
- PECTORAL
- DECAY
- JOULE
- MAGENTA
- PUPIL
- FOETUS
- ASEXUAL
- CANAL
- ADENINE
- BICEPS
- TAIL
- NITRATES
- HABER
- ABDOMEN
- VITREOUS
- MOLAR
- MILK
- SPECIFIC

ANSWERS TO VERTICAL CLUES
1 CHLORO-FLUORO COMPOUNDS
2 AEROSOLS

The Numbers Game

1	7	14	0.34 nm
2	−183°C	15	6
3	4%	16	18
4	4	17	−57 kJ/mole
5	24 dm³	18	78%
6	−273°C	19	105
7	760 mm	20	40
8	37°C	21	270°C
9	19	22	78°C
10	235	23	−196°C
11	250°C	24	10
12	3	25	39
13	170°C	26	16

The Numbers Game

1	96°C	**14**	1
2	1	**15**	8
3	3	**16**	8
4	80	**17**	4
5	40	**18**	1000°C
6	96 500	**19**	8
7	16	**20**	119°C
8	450°C	**21**	373 K
9	21%	**22**	4830°C
10	0	**23**	350°C
11	14	**24**	4.2
12	2	**25**	1840
13	6×10^{23}	**26**	2

True or False

1 T

2 T

3 F Robert Brown observed the movement of pollen grains in water, i.e. Brownian movement.

4 F Carbon dioxide is a linear molecule.

5 T

6 T

7 T

8 F Hydrogen sulphide is colourless.

9 T

10 T

11 F Used to deliver powders.

12 F Calcium carbonate is insoluble.

13 F Coal burns with a smokeless flame under carefully controlled conditions.

14 F Texas has large deposits of sulphur.

15 F Endothermic reactions cause a fall in temperature.

16 T

17 F Saltpetre is potassium nitrate.

18 F Beta particle is an electron.

19 T

20 T

21 T

22 T

23 F Records are made of P.V.C.

24 F P.V.C. is made from an addition polymerisation.

25 F Kineo means moving.

The Wheel

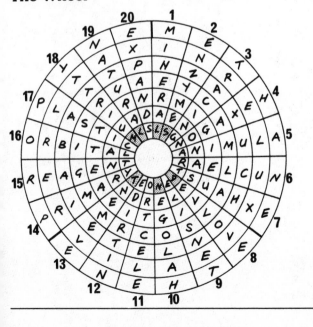

Outer Circle Words
1-7 METHANE
8-13 ETHENE
14-20 PROPYNE

Inner Circle Words
1 REAGENT
2 COSTLY

113

The Wheel

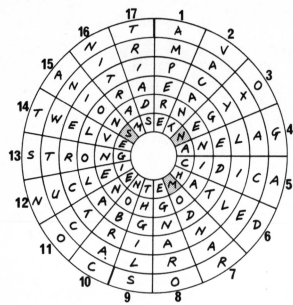

Inner Circle Words
1 SEA
2 EIGHT
3 CEMENT

Outer Circle Words
1-17 AVAGADRO'S CONSTANT

Word Blocks

A
1 CHARLES
2 COLLIDE
3 LINKING
4 CLOTHES
5 AMYLASE
6 PRODUCT
7 CURRENT

D
1 BLOCKS
2 BUNSEN
3 CATION
4 KSHELL
5 CHAINS
6 DILUTE

B
1 FILLING
2 BURNING
3 CERAMIC
4 CYANIDE
5 PROPANE
6 SURFACE
7 BROMINE

E
1 VIOLET
2 LOWEST
3 KELVIN
4 VACUUM
5 STEAMY
6 ZYMASE

C
1 CHOKING
2 BROMINE
3 GREATER
4 ATTACKS
5 KRYPTON
6 BARRIER
7 CHARGED

Answers to Diagonal Clues
A CONTACT
B FURNACE
C CREATED
D BUTENE
E VOLUME

Word Search

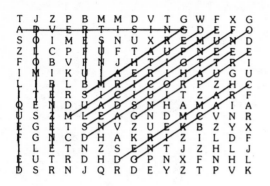

Words to Find

1	ADVERTISING	12	BUFFER
2	ONE THOUSAND	13	MINUS
3	FUNGICIDES	14	PURE
4	DEUTERIUM	15	RATE
5	EMPIRICAL	16	RING
6	LIQUEFIED		
7	CRACKING		
8	DOLOMITE		
9	HAMMERED		
10	BENZENE		
11	GRAHAM'S		

Word Search

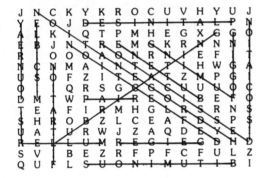

1	HYDROGENATION	11	FOGGING
2	DISSOCIATION	12	BUTENE
3	GEIGER-MULLER	13	MISCIBLE
4	LUBRICATING	14	FUMING
5	DEFLECTION	15	PAIR
6	BITUMINOUS	16	RUST
7	DESSICATOR		
8	FILTRATION		
9	PLATINISED		
10	DOUNREAY		

All the Vowels

1	AERATED	11	RADICALS
2	MANGANESE	12	DISTILLATE
3	PYRAMIDAL	13	BROMOTHYMOL BLUE
4	CARBONATES	14	SULPHATE
5	PERMUTIT	15	LEAD ACID
6	DIVALENT	16	VALENCY
7	MIXED	17	FORWARD
8	BROMIDES	18	VAPORISATION
9	POISONOUS	19	ZERO
10	CONCENTRATED	20	FUNCTIONAL

Missing Letter

THE LAW APPLYING TO CHEMICAL REACTIONS

C DESICCATOR
O FLUORESCENT
N DANIELL
S CAUSTIC SODA
E DISINFECTANTS
R FERMENTATION
V EVAPORATES
A ASPHALT
T DISTILLATION
I AMMONIUM
O CLOSED
N BALLOON

O OLEUM
F DIFFRACTION

E CALORIMETER
N FLINT
E FISSILE
R BATTERY
G GRAHAM'S
Y CYCLES

Missing Letter

G NEGATIVELY
R BECQUEREL
O METHYL ORANGE
U GREENHOUSE
P PHASE
S MIST

P PIPETTE.
E HOMOGENOUS
R AVOGADRO
I CHADWICK
O FOAM
D SOLID
S J J THOMSON

D TIDAL
O MACROMOLECULE
B BLEACHING
E TEAT
R LE CHATELIER
E ESTERIFICATION
I HYDROPHILIC
N MONOCLINIC
E PHENOLPHTHALEIN
R QUARTZ

Solve and Fit

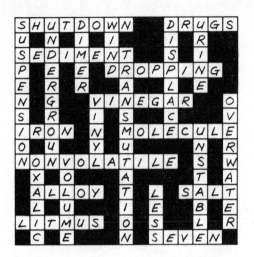

Solve and Fit

Firsts and Seconds

1. PRESSURE
2. HYDROXONIUM
3. ATOMICITY
4. RADIOTHERAPY
5. MOULDED
6. ATTRACT
7. CLASSIFICATION
8. ETHANOIC
9. UNSATURATED
10. TWOTHIRDS
11. INDICATORS
12. CELLULOSE
13. AIRCRAFT
14. LONGTERM
15. RESPIRATION
16. ELECTRONEGATIVE
17. CHLORIDE
18. HEAVIER
19. AMMONIA
20. RADON
21. GIANT
22. ENERGY
23. ABSORB
24. BELOW
25. LITMUS
26. ENTHALPY

Extra Clues for Vertical Words

☐ 1-14 PHARMACEUTICAL
☐ 15-26 RECHARGEABLE
◯ 1-10 RUTHERFORD
◯ 11-21 REFRIGERANT
◯ 22-26 GROUP

Firsts and Seconds

1. MANURE
2. ETHANOL
3. THREE
4. ANTACID
5. LEAST
6. LACQUER
7. OXIDATION
8. INDEPENDENT
9. DECREASE
10. SURFACE
11. MOTION
12. ABOVE
13. LINEAR
14. LSHELL
15. ETHANE
16. ASTON
17. BY-PRODUCT
18. LIGHTNING
19. EQUATION
20. DIAMOND
21. UNREACTIVE
22. CATALYTIC
23. TIMBER
24. INHIBITOR
25. LIMESTONE
26. ENRICHED

Extra Clues for Vertical Words

☐ 1-10 METALLOIDS
☐ 11-19 MALLEABLE
☐ 20-26 DUCTILE
◯ 1-9 ELECTRONS
◯ 10-17 COVALENT
◯ 18-26 IONIC BOND

Bits and Pieces

1. ANTHRACITE
2. DECANT
3. DESICCATOR
4. IDE
5. TRIGONAL
6. IDEALGAS
7. OSTWALD
8. NITRIC
9. COLLOID
10. OUTER
11. NODULES
12. DIMER
13. ENDOTHERMIC
14. NYLON
15. SLAG
16. AROMATIC
17. TUNGSTEN
18. INTERMOLECULAR
19. OCTET
20. NON-RENEWABLE

Remaining Letters Phrase
TWO TYPES OF POLYMERISATION

Vertical Words
ADDITION
CONDENSATION

Bits and Pieces

1. ACETONE
2. THOMSON
3. ORGANIC
4. MOLARITY
5. IONISATION
6. CLEAVAGE
7. THERMOMETER
8. HYDROXIDE
9. EMPIRICAL
10. OXONIUM
11. RAMSAY
12. YIELD
13. OILY
14. FOREIGN
15. MONOVALENT
16. ATMOSPHERE
17. TITRATION
18. TRANSFER
19. ELECTRICITY
20. RAYON

Extra Clue, Vertical Words
ATOMIC THEORY OF MATTER

Remaining Letters Words
JOHN DALTON

Twos and Threes

Twos and Threes

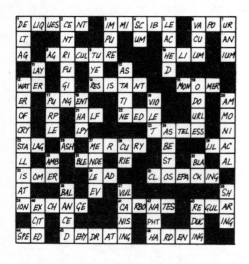

Missing Letter

1 FUME
2 BEAKER
3 EVAPORATING
4 CUPBOARD
5 TRIPOD
6 INVERTED
7 BOSS CLAMP
8 ANODE
9 PLATINUM
10 BURETTE

11 BEEHIVE
12 FUNNEL
13 GAUZE
14 CENTRIFUGE
15 IGNITION
16 FUNNEL
17 BUNG
18 MEASURING
19 CONICAL
20 FLASK

21 CYLINDER
22 DELIVERY
23 CATHODE
24 VOLUMETRIC
25 SYRINGE
26 PIPETTE
27 TAP
28 PUMP
29 THISTLE
30 RETORT

Extra Clues, Vertical Words
1-19 FRACTIONATING COLUMN
20-30 FILTER PAPER

The Numbers Game

1	2	3	4	5	6	7	8	9	10	11	12	13	14	15
D	I	M	N	Q	U	A	L	G	B	E	T	O	J	K

16	17	18	19	20	21	22	23	24	25	26	27	28	29	30
P	R	S	W	X	Y	Z	V	AA	BB	H	CC	F	DD	C

Solve and Fit

A Mix-Up

1	2	3	4	5	6	7	8	9	10	11	12	13	14	15
L	R	Y	A	B	N	P	DD	X	T	W	M	BB	S	G

16	17	18	19	20	21	22	23	24	25	26	27	28	29	30
C	Z	AA	Q	CC	D	J	K	H	U	I	V	O	F	E

Bits and Pieces

1. SPLITRING
2. ALTERNATOR
3. THERMIONIC
4. EYEPIECE
5. LINEAR
6. LATENT
7. INWARD
8. THERMAL
9. ELECTROSCOPE
10. SECONDARY
11. EBONITE
12. LOSS
13. LAMP
14. IONISED
15. PARALLAX
16. TRANSFORMER
17. INSULATOR
18. COMMUTATOR
19. AMPLITUDE
20. LENS
21. OSCILLATE
22. RESOLUTION
23. BICONCAVE
24. IONOSPHERE
25. TEMPORARY

Extra Clue, Vertical Words

SATELLITE'S ELLIPTICAL ORBIT

The remaining letters spell out OVAL IN SHAPE

Firsts and Seconds

1. COEFFICIENT
2. ATMOSPHERIC
3. PROPULSION
4. ATTENUATION
5. COMPLEMENTARY
6. INCLINATION
7. TICKERTAPE
8. AXIS
9. NUMBER
10. CURVATURE
11. EARTH
12. GRADUATED
13. AMPERE
14. LEAD
15. VIBRATE
16. ACCELERATION
17. NORTHSEEKING
18. OILFILLED
19. MECHANICAL
20. ELECTRICAL
21. THERMODYNAMICS
22. ENGLAND
23. RECTANGLE

Extra Clues

☐ 1-11 CAPACITANCE
12-23 GALVANOMETER
○ 1-4 THIN
5-13 ALTIMETER
14-23 ARTIFICIAL

A Mix-Up Units and Prefixes

1	2	3	4	5	6	7	8	9	10	11	12
D	H	N	A	K	P	S	M	Q	F	L	U
HH	DD	NN	KK	TT	PP	RR	LL	UU	WW	II	OO

13	14	15	16	17	18	19	20	21	22	23
J	I	O	G	R	E	T	V	B	W	C
FF	EE	SS	BB	QQ	MM	VV	GG	AA	JJ	CC

Missing Letter

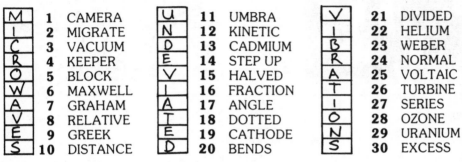

1 CAMERA	11 UMBRA	21 DIVIDED
2 MIGRATE	12 KINETIC	22 HELIUM
3 VACUUM	13 CADMIUM	23 WEBER
4 KEEPER	14 STEP UP	24 NORMAL
5 BLOCK	15 HALVED	25 VOLTAIC
6 MAXWELL	16 FRACTION	26 TURBINE
7 GRAHAM	17 ANGLE	27 SERIES
8 RELATIVE	18 DOTTED	28 OZONE
9 GREEK	19 CATHODE	29 URANIUM
10 DISTANCE	20 BENDS	30 EXCESS

Vertical words
1 MICROWAVES
2 UNDEVIATED
3 VIBRATIONS

Double Puzzle

Extra Clues

First word: DECLINATION
Second word: MODERATOR

Reference Check

Answer grid

1 DISPLACEMENT
2 EXPANSION
3 COMBUSTION
4 LIGHTNESS
5 INTERFERE
6 NOPARALLAX
7 ANTICLOCKWISE
8 THOUSAND
9 IRREGULAR
10 OPEN
11 NEUTRALISE
12 MACROSCOPIC
13 OPTICAL
14 DEMAGNETISATION
15 EVAPORATES
16 RECIPROCAL
17 ALUMINIUM
18 TIMEBASE
19 OUTWARD
20 REFRACTIVE

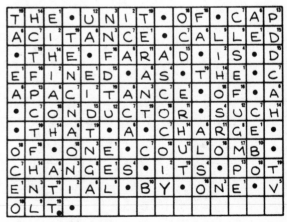

THE UNIT OF CAPACITANCE CALLED THE FARAD IS DEFINED AS THE CAPACITANCE OF A CONDUCTOR SUCH THAT A CHARGE OF ONE COULOMB CHANGES ITS POTENTIAL BY ONE VOLT.

An A.B.C. Crossword

The Wheel

PUZZLE 50

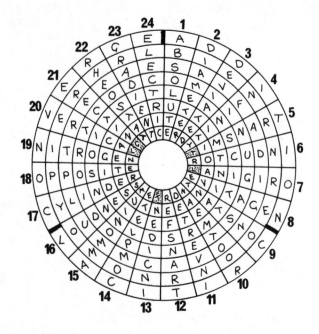

Outer Circle Answers
1-8 ADDITION
9-16 CRITICAL
17-24 CONVERGE

Inner Circle Answers
1 DENSE
2 METRE
3 RADIO
4 RATIO
5 COUNT
6 RAY

Word Blocks

A

1. SPRING
2. SCREEN
3. BRAKES
4. ANGLES
5. APPEAR
6. BIGGER

B

1. CENTRE
2. HUMOUR
3. ERRORS
4. CONVEX
5. MAGNET
6. LINKED

C

1. VAPOUR
2. ROTATE
3. TILTED
4. LIQUID
5. DYNAMO
6. REMOVE

D

1. CHARGE
2. PASCAL
3. STRONG
4. DOUBLE
5. MOTION
6. NEWTON

E

1. ROCKET
2. DEGREE
3. HIDDEN
4. VACUUM
5. EFFECT
6. BUBBLE

The Diagonal Words are
A SCALAR, **B** CURVED,
C VOLUME, **D** CARBON,
E REDUCE.

Word Blocks

A

1. SURFACE
2. CHARGED
3. BRUSHES
4. BATTERY
5. AMMETER
6. BETWEEN
7. ANGULAR

B

1. CONTROL
2. BOILING
3. OSMOTIC
4. SLOPING
5. AVERAGE
6. DIFFUSE
7. DEGREES

C

1. FORMULA
2. FILINGS
3. VISIBLE
4. CRYSTAL
5. BRAKING
6. ALCOHOL
7. TENSION

D

1. PRIMARY
2. MAXIMUM
3. UPRIGHT
4. VOLTAGE
5. WASHING
6. UNEQUAL
7. VIRTUAL

The Diagonal Words are
A SHUTTER, **B** COMPASS,
C FISSION, **D** PARTIAL.

Word Blocks

A

1. ANODE
2. BLACK
3. PULSE
4. BORON
5. RELAY

B

1. CHAIN
2. FOCUS
3. MAINS
4. SMALL
5. CROSS

C

1. POWER
2. FLOAT
3. GLASS
4. SALTS
5. FORCE

D

1. LIGHT
2. RANGE
3. CURVE
4. GAUGE
5. SLOPE

E

1. SOLID
2. SPOUT
3. STEAM
4. SCREW
5. CLOUD

F

1. THUMB
2. TOUCH
3. WATER
4. METAL
5. LEVEL

The Diagonal Words are
A ALLOY, **B** COILS,
C PLATE, **D** LARGE,
E SPEED, **F** TOTAL.

Word Blocks

The Diagonal Words are
A BALANCED, **B** SPECTRUM,
C FRICTION, **D** MOLECULE.

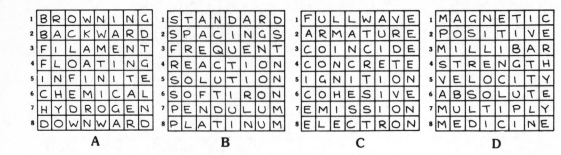

A

1	BROWNING
2	BACKWARD
3	FILAMENT
4	FLOATING
5	INFINITE
6	CHEMICAL
7	HYDROGEN
8	DOWNWARD

B

1	STANDARD
2	SPACINGS
3	FREQUENT
4	REACTION
5	SOLUTION
6	SOFTIRON
7	PENDULUM
8	PLATINUM

C

1	FULLWAVE
2	ARMATURE
3	COINCIDE
4	CONCRETE
5	IGNITION
6	COHESIVE
7	EMISSION
8	ELECTRON

D

1	MAGNETIC
2	POSITIVE
3	MILLIBAR
4	STRENGTH
5	VELOCITY
6	ABSOLUTE
7	MULTIPLY
8	MEDICINE

Twos and Threes

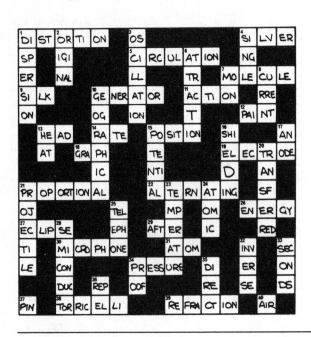

Doubles and Trebles

1	CLOCK	**15**	MERCURY
2	MOTOR	**16**	RECTIFIED
3	PAPER	**17**	REACTOR
4	VALVE	**18**	SLIP-RING
5	AMPERE	**19**	DIAMONDS
6	BREEZE	**20**	HALF-WAVE
7	COPPER	**21**	PARABOLA
8	HAMMER	**22**	PARALLEL
9	MATTER	**23**	HYDRO-ELECTRIC
10	MEDIUM	**24**	MAGNETITE
11	OUTPUT	**25**	HEMISPHERES
12	STATIC	**26**	PERPENDICULAR
13	BALANCE	**27**	PERISCOPE
14	CIRCUIT	**28**	PERMANENT

The Numbers Game

1	10^{18} km	**16**	27.3 days
2	89%	**17**	10^{10} km
3	10^{23} km	**18**	6,000°C
4	4	**19**	100,000,000
5	150,000,000 km	**20**	300,000 km
6	100 metres	**21**	45 seconds
7	13,000 km	**22**	500,000,000 km
8	10^{-7}m	**23**	70
9	4 light years	**24**	99%
10	50,000,000 km	**25**	80%
11	9	**26**	14,000,000°C
12	1 year	**27**	700
13	250 years	**28**	105
14	3	**29**	23%
15	100 billion	**30**	46

The Numbers Game

1	47 m/s	**16**	3,600,000
2	0.08	**17**	100N/m^2
3	21%	**18**	240
4	78%	**19**	760 mm
5	330 m/s	**20**	250 mm
6	30 m/s	**21**	1013
7	0.9%	**22**	30A
8	500 m/s	**23**	3A
9	11,000 m/s	**24**	13A
10	300,000,000 m/s	**25**	0.75
11	193,000	**26**	10^{-10}m
12	13 m/s	**27**	27 m/s
13	1.6×10^{-19}	**28**	3×10^{-2}m
14	10N	**29**	20 Hz
15	9.8 m/s^2	**30**	20,000 Hz

Famous Scientists

1	2	3	4	5	6	7	8	9
F	J	G	R	Q	M	K	D	B

10	11	12	13	14	15	16	17	18
N	L	O	C	H	E	P	A	I

Famous Scientists

A	B	C	D	E	F	G	H	I	J	K	L	M
26	7	13	9	12	2	11	3	25	1	14	5	10

N	O	P	Q	R	S	T	U	V	W	X	Y	Z
17	4	18	6	20	16	8	22	15	24	19	23	21

REVISION NOTES

REVISION NOTES

REVISION NOTES

REVISION NOTES